T0419496

EDUCATION IN A COMPETITIVE AND GLOBALIZING WORLD

THE ROLE OF HIGHER EDUCATION IN INNOVATION AND ENTREPRENEURSHIP

EDUCATION IN A COMPETITIVE AND GLOBALIZING WORLD

Additional books in this series can be found on Nova's website under the Series tab.

Additional e-books in this series can be found on Nova's website under the e-book tab.

EDUCATION IN A COMPETITIVE AND GLOBALIZING WORLD

THE ROLE OF HIGHER EDUCATION IN INNOVATION AND ENTREPRENEURSHIP

ARMANDO M. CLINTON
EDITOR

For permission to use material from this book please contact us:
Telephone 631-231-7269; Fax 631-231-8175
Web Site: http://www.novapublishers.com

Additional color graphics may be available in the e-book version of this book.

Library of Congress Cataloging-in-Publication Data

ISBN: 978-1-63321-176-6

Published by Nova Science Publishers, Inc. † New York

CONTENTS

PREFACE

This report shows how colleges and universities nationwide are supporting innovation and entrepreneurship in order to strengthen regional economies, create jobs and keep America competitive.

The report highlights efforts in five key areas:

* Promoting student innovation and entrepreneurship;
* Encouraging faculty innovation and entrepreneurship;
* Actively supporting university technology transfer;
* Facilitating university-industry collaboration; and,
* Engaging in regional and local economic development efforts.

In: The Role of Higher Education in Innovation ISBN: 978-1-63321-176-6
Editor: Armando M. Clinton

Chapter 1

THE INNOVATIVE AND ENTREPRENEURIAL UNIVERSITY: HIGHER EDUCATION, INNOVATION AND ENTREPRENEURSHIP IN FOCUS*

Office of Innovation & Entrepreneurship, Economic Development Administration†

FOREWORD

Innovation is a key driver of economic growth in the United States. At the Department of Commerce, our agencies and bureaus are focused on nurturing innovation, developing advanced manufacturing in the United States, and increasing exports to the world. Innovation is a priority for the U.S. Department of Commerce because it helps American industry, universities, and research institutes to develop the next generation of technologies and increase the number of high-growth American startups.

Over the last several months, the Department of Commerce's Office of Innovation and Entrepreneurship spoke directly to colleges and universities

---

* This is an edited, reformatted and augmented version of a report prepared in consultation with the National Advisory Council on Innovation and Entrepreneurship. It was released by the U.S. Department of Commerce, October 2013.

† Author Note: The Office of Innovation & Entrepreneurship is part of the Economic Development Administration.

around the country to understand how they are nurturing and promoting innovation and entrepreneurship. This effort was conducted in response to a letter that was marshaled by the National Advisory Council on Innovation and Entrepreneurship to the Department in 2011, which described how university-based innovation and entrepreneurship is blossoming, and outlining steps that the university community would like the US government to take to further nurture economic value creation in conjunction with universities. This report entitled, "The Innovative and Entrepreneurial University: Higher Education, Innovation and Entrepreneurship in Focus," includes the results of those interviews and conversations.

In 2009, the National Advisory Council on Innovation and Entrepreneurship was created as part of the implementation of the America COMPETES Act. This council, comprised of some of America's leading entrepreneurs, investors and university leaders, has been a tremendous asset to the Administration by providing ideas and feedback on policies that nurture innovation and entrepreneurship. Over the last two years, the Council, under the leadership of co-chairs Steve Case, Dr. Mary Sue Coleman and Dr. Desh Deshpande, has had a major impact on several Administration accomplishments including Startup America, the American JOBS Act, and a letter from university presidents that was the starting point of this report.

That letter, entitled "Recommendations to Facilitate University-Based Technology Commercialization", mobilized the higher education community. It provided a strategic framework for universities, colleges, and its partners in government, philanthropy, and business to advance university-based innovation and entrepreneurship. This framework has become part of the discussion on campuses everywhere as higher education thinks about its future and the desires of its students, faculty, and communities. Signed by 142 of America's leading universities, this letter spawned similar efforts by community colleges, state colleges, Historically Black Colleges and Universities (HCBUs), and several government research laboratories.

The Department's Office of Innovation and Entrepreneurship spoke directly to nearly every signatory of this letter. As expected, we found that universities and colleges across America are engaged in an exciting and comprehensive set of programs to nurture innovation and entrepreneurship among their students, faculty and communities with the goal of supporting industry and the regional economy. While their approaches vary based on geography, history and size, they are all committed to the innovation economy and the role of entrepreneurs in driving that economy. In addition, the universities are all strong partners of the U.S. government, its research agencies, and the U.S. Department of Commerce.

Moving forward, the Department will work collaboratively with our partners in higher education to develop a common action plan to support and nurture university-based innovation and entrepreneurship. The insights in this report provide a significant starting point for the development of this action plan on the roles of universities and the federal government in nurturing innovation and entrepreneurship to support America's economy.

REMARKS FROM THE CO-CHAIRS OF THE NATIONAL ADVISORY COUNCIL ON INNOVATION AND ENTREPRENEURSHIP

The co-chairs of the National Advisory Council on Innovation and Entrepreneurship (NACIE), and on behalf of the full membership, would like to thank the U.S. Department of Commerce for its follow up work with universities, national labs, community colleges and Historically Black Colleges and Universities.

Since its inception, NACIE has focused on the issue of the commercialization of federally-funded research, and the opportunity to create economic value and jobs in the United States through greater commercialization by our university, lab and corporate research partners. In April 2011, four of our members led the charge to engage universities directly in this effort. Through the combined efforts of Presidents' Mary Sue Coleman, Bud Peterson, Michael Crow, and Chancellor Holden Thorp, and the outside support of several higher education groups, we submitted a letter to the U.S. Department of Commerce focused on university-based innovation and entrepreneurship. America's higher education institutions are engaged in a variety of exciting programs to nurture innovation and entrepreneurship as part of the education of their students, faculty and alumni, and as a tool to leverage their assets to create economic value in their communities. The letter emphasized key steps taken by the higher education community to enhance those programs, and suggested ways in which the federal government could enhance it even more. While there are certain characteristics that all the universities share, this report highlights the diversity of programs across the United States in a way that reflects the diversity of size, geography, culture and research capacity of our higher education institutions.

This report is the start of similar outreach by the U.S. Department of Commerce and other federal agencies to universities, federal labs and private companies to better understand the nature of our innovation and our capacity to commercialize. In addition, NACIE looks forward to promoting the ideas in this report and to promote those that can be replicated for greatest impact. We know that these activities will lead to greater innovation, commercialization, and broad-based entrepreneurship from our university communities.

We look forward to continued involvement with the U.S. Department of Commerce and to making future recommendations in this area as well as other critical areas of importance to NACIE, including access to capital and the celebration of entrepreneurship in the United States.

Co-Chairs

Steve Case
Chairman & CEO
Revolution LLC

Dr. Mary Sue Coleman
President
University of Michigan

Dr. Gururaj Deshpande
Chairman
Sparta Group

Members

Tom Alberg
Managing Director
Madrona Venture Group

James Andrew
Chief Strategy & Innovation Officer
Koninklijke Philips N.V.

Tom Baruch
Founder
Formation8 Capital

Dr. Claude Canizares
Vice President for Research, Associate Provost
Massachusetts Institute of Technology

Dr. Curtis Carlson
President & CEO
SRI International

Robin Chase
Founder
Buzzcar

Marcelo Claure
Chairman, President & CEO
Brightstar

Dr. Michael Crow
President
Arizona State University

Ping Fu
VP & Chief Strategy Officer
3D Systems Corporation

Dr. Christina Gabriel
President
University Energy Partnership

Dr. Barron Harvey
Dean
Howard University School of Business

Krisztina Holly
Former Vice Provost for Innovation
University of Southern California

Ray Leach
CEO
Jumpstart

Kenneth Morse
Managing Director
Entrepreneurship Ventures

Dr. G.P. "Bud" Peterson
President
Georgia Institute of Technology

Michael Roberts
CEO
The Roberts Companies

RoseAnn B. Rosenthal
President & CEO
Ben Franklin Technology Partners of Southeastern Pennsylvania

Dr. Holden Thorp
Provost
Washington University in St. Louis

Dr. Charles Vest
Former President
National Academy of Engineering

Dr. Jeffrey Wadsworth
CEO
Battelle

Office of Innovation & Entrepreneurship

Nish Acharya
Former Director & Senior Advisor to the Secretary

Gautam Prakash
Acting Director

Heidi Lovett
ELDP Research Team

Asif Alvi
ELDP Research Team

O. Felix Obi
Intern

Cassandra Ingram
Economist

Paul Corson
Former Deputy Director

Brandi Parker
Senior Policy Advisor

Steven Rutz
ELDP Research Team

Marc Liverman
ELDP Research Team

Amy Nasr
Intern

Lauren Dupuis
EDA Management Analyst

Kari McNair
Research Analyst

Saliha Loucif
ELDP Research Team

Shari Stout
ELDP Research Team

Kyle Ward
ELDP Research Team

Nithyaa Venkataramani
Intern

Bryan Clubb
Intern

ACKNOWLEDGMENTS

This report would not have been possible without a sustained effort by many individuals and organizations that deeply care about universities, commercialization, innovation, and entrepreneurship.

Foremost, we at the Office of Innovation and Entrepreneurship (OIE) would like to thank the National Advisory Council on Innovation and Entrepreneurship (NACIE) for its leadership in many areas since its inception in 2010. NACIE members have been critical in advising the U.S. Department of Commerce and its federal agency partners about the importance of innovation and entrepreneurship. In particular, the four major university presidents in NACIE were our key contacts to the university community. We would like to thank Dr. Mary Sue Coleman, Dr. Michael Crow, Dr. Bud Peterson, and Dr. Holden Thorp for their leadership in the creation of the letter to former Secretary Gary Locke on "Recommendations to Facilitate University-Based Technology Commercialization" and support of our subsequent follow-up. This letter has become an important resource for universities and colleges around the country as they plan and develop their innovation and entrepreneurship programs. It is often cited within the academic community for its thoroughness in outlining the role of universities in innovation, and entrepreneurship.

In addition, OIE owes tremendous gratitude to several associations representing higher education, innovation and entrepreneurship. These organizations have long advocated for greater federal support for research and development (R&D) as well as for greater commercialization. Most notably, the American Association of Universities (AAU) and the Association of Public

Land Grant Universities (APLU) have been dedicated partners since the beginning of this effort. These associations helped NACIE to marshal the original 142 signatories for the NACIE University Presidents' letter.

Several other higher education associations also supported our effort through outreach to their members. In particular, associations representing institutions at the state and regional level worked with us to understand their members' approaches to innovation and entrepreneurship and to highlight their strategies–which we found were often similar to those at the major research universities. The American Association of State Colleges and Universities (AASCU) connected us with over 60 state universities and hosted a number of forums from which we obtained valuable insights. The National Association of Community College Entrepreneurship (NACCE), has over 170 community college members that have made a similar commitment to entrepreneurship as part of the Startup America Initiative commitment. And the United Negro College Fund and the Historically Black Colleges and Universities' (HBCU) Deans Summit helped us reached out to their member schools, which are looking at developing entrepreneurship programs around the technical programs they have historically had and around social innovation. We also received support and encouragement from the Association of University Technology Managers (AUTM), the American Council on Education (ACE), and the National Council on Entrepreneurial Tech Transfer (NCET2). We look forward to working more closely with them in the future.

We would like to acknowledge the work of many members of the U.S. Department of Commerce family who have provided support and encouragement of university-based innovation and entrepreneurship. Additionally, we received support and encouragement from the Office of the Secretary, the leadership of the U.S. Economic Development Administration (EDA), the U.S. Patent and Trademark Office (USPTO), the U.S. National Institute of Standards and Technology (NIST), the Department of Commerce's Executive Leadership Development Program (ELDP), and of course, the staff and supporters of OIE.

Office of Innovation and Entrepreneurship
July 2013

EXECUTIVE SUMMARY

America's colleges and universities have gotten the entrepreneurial bug. From the i6 Proof of Concept Center at the University of Akron to the University of Wyoming's Technology Business Center, America's higher education institutions are embracing the importance of innovation, commercialization, entrepreneurship, and the creation of economic value for their communities. Most people are familiar with the traditional centers of university-based innovation and entrepreneurship such as the Massachusetts Institute of Technology (MIT) and its connection to the Greater Boston entrepreneurship ecosystem. But over the last decade, more universities, community colleges, Historically Black Colleges and Universities (HCBU), and regional state colleges have embraced innovation and entrepreneurship as critical to their mission and role in their communities.

In 2011, 142 major research universities and associations submitted a letter to the Secretary of Commerce renewing their commitment to innovation and entrepreneurship on campus and in their communities, and asked the federal government to continue to work with them in these areas. This report is the next step in a two-year effort by the U.S. Department of Commerce and the National Advisory Council on Innovation and Entrepreneurship (NACIE) to understand exactly what America's colleges and universities are doing programmatically and strategically to nurture innovation, commercialization, and entrepreneurship among students, faculty, alumni, and within their communities.

In order to determine what efforts the signatories have made in innovation and entrepreneurship, representatives from the Office of Innovation and Entrepreneurship (OIE) spoke to the leaders of 131 research universities, located around the United States. OIE also collected information from community colleges, regional colleges, and HBCUs about their programs. Time and again, the leadership at these universities and colleges emphasized the pedagogical value of entrepreneurship, their vision for entrepreneurship in their communities, and the organizational infrastructure they are developing to maximize the research, ideas, and talent associated with their colleges and universities. The results from these discussions will encourage anyone concerned about America's capacity to innovate and create the next generation of high-growth startups, especially those who feel that institutions of higher education have an important role to play in this arena.

Over the last two decades, the majority of job creation in the United States has occurred in young, startup companies.[1] In addition, innovation, and the real-world application of that innovation, is all around us. From breakthroughs in medicine and genetics to clean technologies, social media, or education technologies, innovation is becoming a more critical part of all of the products and services available today. While the United States remains the global leader in innovation and entrepreneurship, there is constant competition from around the world to maintain that leadership.

And as global competition continues to grow, it is critical that the institutions driving innovation improve their ability to develop products and services with market relevance and economic value. Historically, a large portion of America's investments in innovative companies have been centered in the metropolitan regions of San Francisco/Silicon Valley, CA; Greater Boston, MA; New York/New Jersey; Austin, TX; Seattle, WA; Washington D.C., and San Diego, CA.[2] However, universities outside of these areas are now leading the charge to model new entrepreneurial ecosystems. This is best exemplified by the University of Michigan's efforts in Michigan, Arizona State University's impact in the Phoenix area, the University of Akron's work in Ohio, and the University of Southern California's efforts in the Los Angeles area. In addition, hundreds of colleges and universities across the U.S. are creating entrepreneurship programs with the short-term objective of creating educational value for their students and the long-term objective of driving economic growth in their communities through locally-developed enterprises.

Nearly all of the university leaders that participated in the discussion emphasized the importance of the U.S. government and the university community working together to maximize innovation commercialization. Over the last decade, universities have been the largest sector to receive federal R&D grants –receiving nearly $36 billion from federal agencies in FY2009.[3] Universities have received funding and assistance from a variety of federal agencies, including the Departments of Commerce, Education, Agriculture, Labor, State, Health and Human Services, Energy, Defense, U.S. Agency for

---

[1] Haltiwanger, John C., Ron S. Jarmin, and Javier Miranda, "Who Creates Jobs? Small vs. Large vs. Young," NBER Working Paper No. 16300, August 2010, see http://www.nber.org /papers/w16300.pdf?new_window=1

[2] PricewaterhouseCoopers and National Venture Capital Association, "Investments by Stage of Development Q1 1995- Q2 2012," MoneyTree Report, see https://www. pwcmoneytree.com /MTPublic/ns/nav.jsp%3Fpage=notice&iden=B

[3] National Science Foundation, "Science and Engineering Indicators, 2012," See http://www.nsf. gov/statistics/digest12/portfolio.cfm#4 and http:// www.nsf.gov/ statistics /digest12 /funding.cfm#3.

International Development (USAID) and the National Science Foundation (NSF). In short, universities and the U.S. government are key partners in research, development, and innovation. Furthermore, leaders of universities and federal agencies share a common desire to increase collaboration and bring innovative ideas and research to the market to create real-world solutions and high-growth startups.

The NACIE University Presidents' letter, "Recommendations to Facilitate University-Based Technology Commercialization" identified five focus categories at the heart of the innovation and entrepreneurship activities within America's universities. These categories are student entrepreneurship, faculty entrepreneurship, technology transfer, industry collaboration, and engagement in regional economic development. The universities affiliated with the letter are each addressing innovation and entrepreneurship in diverse ways relevant to their research budgets and programs, student population, geography, history, and culture. Through their distinct approaches, these institutions hope to improve their own partnerships with the federal government and pursue their broader organizational goals. Following are summaries of some of the best practices and emerging trends at universities and colleges.

Promoting Student Innovation and Entrepreneurship

Colleges and universities are investing heavily in the development of their students' entrepreneurial skills. While many students dream of starting the next Facebook® or Twitter® (both of which were started by students), universities are more focused on the pedagogical value of entrepreneurship as a set of skills that can be applied across professional environments and activities to supplement the students' classroom experience. Universities are investing both in formal programs as well as in extra-curricular activities to channel students' interest in solving global problems through entrepreneurship. Examples of formal programs include degrees and certificates in entrepreneurship, while examples of extra-curricular activities include business plan contests, entrepreneurship clubs, and startup internships. Many universities are even experimenting with on-campus accelerators, entrepreneurial dorms, and student venture funds. At the very least, these activities provide critical organizational skills to students, and at the very best, may create the next great university spinoff. Some of the most effective practices include:

The University of Colorado System's Innovation and Entrepreneur Degree Program – Offers a Bachelor's degree in Innovation (B.I.), through a unique multi-disciplinary team and course work approach.

The University of Illinois' Patent Clinic – Provides law students the opportunity to draft patent applications for student inventors.

Washington University in St. Louis' student internship program – Offers 25 paid internships per summer for students to work in a start-up's.

Rice University – Raised and provided $1.2 million in cash and in-kind services for its business plan contest in 2011. This money has served as a de-facto angel round of funding for the recipient companies.

University of Washington – Hosts a multi-level business plan competition comprising of different competitions throughout the school year, in combination with seminars, courses, and mentorship to assist in pushing student ideas to the next level.

University of Florida- "INSPIREation" Hall – Is the nation's first entrepreneurship-based academic residential community - encouraging student interaction with fellow students, leading researchers, distinguished faculty, business professionals, and entrepreneurs.

Encouraging Faculty Innovation and Entrepreneurship

Faculty and doctoral graduate students conduct the research powering many of the innovations that spawn high-growth startups. However, even at our nation's most entrepreneurial universities, many faculty and graduate students do not always consider the market and societal relevance of their research. To address this issue, universities are putting in place a series of policy changes to encourage more faculty entrepreneurship, which in turn will complement the student entrepreneurship. These changes include greater recognition of faculty entrepreneurs, integrating entrepreneurship into the faculty tenure and selection process, and increasing faculty connections to outside partners - through externships, engagement with business, and targeted resources for startup creation. Finally, universities are actively working with federal agencies to address some of the regulatory challenges around faculty entrepreneurship, in particular, those related to conflict of interest and national security issues. Some of the most effective practices include:

The University of Pittsburgh – Offers a Business of Innovation Commercialization course aimed at educating and motivating both student and faculty researchers in innovation development, commercialization, and entrepreneurship.

University of Southern California – Promotes faculty entrepreneurship and innovation by supporting, rewarding, and funding the work of faculty members.

University of Virginia – In 2010, the University's School of Medicine was among the first to include commercialization and entrepreneurship activities among its promotion and tenure criteria.

University of Nebraska Medical Center's Entrepreneur in Residence (EIR) – The EIR works with licensing staff and researchers at the University of Nebraska's Medical Center to help identify, evaluate, develop, and support the creation of new companies based on UNMC innovations.

Actively Supporting the University Technology Transfer Function

University Technology Transfer Offices (TTO) and Technology Licensing Offices (TLO) have traditionally been the hubs within universities where innovators and outside business leaders engage to commercialize inventions. The recent burst of entrepreneurship on campuses has greatly expanded the role of the TTOs and TLOs. Instead of merely focusing on the commercialization of individual technologies, these offices now act as a central point where students, faculty, alumni, entrepreneurs, investors, and industry can connect with each other. These offices are now focused on identifying and supporting entrepreneurship on campus, helping startups find the best opportunities and building successful business models, changing the culture of their universities, and creating companies that will be based in the communities around the university. TTOs and TLOs have also expanded support beyond their traditional areas, such as energy and life sciences, into education, social innovation, and agriculture. Some of the most effective practices include:

Utah State University's Intellectual Property Services – A university unit within the Commercial Enterprises office that is dedicated to helping faculty and staff manage and protect and commercialize university intellectual property and support institutions in the surrounding areas.

University of North Carolina Chapel Hill's Technology Transfer Internships – Offers internship and fellowship opportunities for students within the TTO.

Cornell University's IP&Pizza™ and IP&Pasta™ – Is an outreach activity for faculty, research staff, and students to increase appreciation of the importance of making university research results useful to society and provide a basic knowledge and understanding of intellectual property issues and an awareness of capturing and protecting valuable intellectual property and its importance to entice potential industry partners.

California Institute of Technology (CalTech) – Files a provisional patent application for every single disclosure that goes through their TTO and later evaluates the technical and business merits over the first year.

Regional Tech Transfer Centers – Serve the needs of research institutions and non-profits throughout a region and are of particular benefit to institutions without TTOs or TLOs. Examples include the South Texas Technology Management Center, the University of Utah, and the Massachusetts Technology Transfer Center. These have been particularly useful for institutions with entrepreneurial faculty but without large TTOs.

Facilitating University-Industry Collaboration

Businesses and industry benefit greatly from university research and innovation. Universities are constantly looking for ways to connect their research and students' education to emerging industry interests. In recent years, universities have put greater emphasis on supporting startup companies, while continuing to engage established companies that have traditionally been their licensing partners. To facilitate greater collaboration and innovation, universities are opening up their facilities, faculty, and students to businesses (small and large) in the hopes of creating greater economic value. Universities are strategically partnering with companies, offering internships and externships, sharing facilities with startups, such as accelerators, and creating venture funds and incentive programs funded by industry, all of which drive increased innovation and product development by university students, faculty, and staff. Some of the most effective practices include:

Clemson University's International Center for Automotive Research (CU-ICAR) – Is an advanced-technology research campus where university, industry, and government organizations collaborate.

University of Minnesota's Industrial Partnership for Research in Interfacial and Materials Engineering (IPrime) – Is a university-industry partnership based on two-way knowledge transfer. The partnership is a consortium of more than 40 companies supporting fundamental and collaborative research on materials.

University of Delaware's Office of Economic Innovation & Partnership (OEIP) – Has established partnerships with the College of Engineering and the Lerner College of Business to establish a program entitled Spin InTM. The program works with local entrepreneurs who 'spin in' a technology, patent, or product that needs further technical development.

Georgia Institute of Technology's (Georgia Tech) Flashpoint – Is a startup accelerator that offers entrepreneurial education and access to experienced mentors, experts, and investors in an immersive, shared-learning, open workspace.

Engaging with Regional and Local Economic Development Efforts

Historically, local economic development has been an important mission of the nation's large universities. Many of America's leading universities, particularly land-grant universities, have always felt a strong responsibility for the betterment of their surrounding communities. These days, universities are increasingly focusing on innovation and entrepreneurship as key contributors to the growth and success of local communities. Universities are requesting the federal government to include commercialization and innovation-driven economic development in their grant programs. In addition, regional economic development planning now often starts with an assessment of a local university's research strengths. In turn, universities are seeking partners to supplement their strengths and overcome their weaknesses through partnerships with community colleges, non-profit economic development agencies, governments, and entrepreneurship groups. Some universities, such as Tulane University, are asking their students and faculty to contribute to local community development through service and projects. Others, such as North Carolina State University, are building innovation-driven campuses that help surrounding cities and communities prosper. Some of the most effective practices include:

Tulane University's Social Innovation and Entrepreneurship Program – Integrates the university with the surrounding economic ecosystem, thereby contributing to local economic development. Students are required to engage outside the campus with the community, often through entrepreneurial projects.
Purdue University's Technical Assistance Projects – Brings faculty and graduate students together to provide cost-free consulting and assistance to local entrepreneurs on business and technical issues.
University of Georgia's Service-Learning Program – Offers enhanced courses incorporating service learning opportunities into all of the University's schools and colleges to increase student involvement in their local communities.
University of Kansas' RedTire's Initiative – Helps link graduate students and alumni with struggling local small/medium-sized businesses. Through a collaborative effort, these businesses receive support and mentorship.

We have learned a great deal from our discussions with university and college leadership. While one size does not fit all, there is certainly something for everyone in this report. It highlights the most interesting and creative programs in each of the five categories summarized above. The goal is for universities and colleges to look at these examples for inspiration and relevance to their programs and objectives. The innovative and entrepreneurial university is the aggregation of all of the great efforts identified in this report, and it is exciting that many institutions are already engaged in a number of these efforts.

Higher education clearly has made great strides in expanding America's innovative capacity. Their innovation and entrepreneurship efforts converge with similar efforts being pursued by the federal government. For example, President Obama issued an Executive Memorandum in October 2011, entitled "Accelerating Technology Transfer and Commercialization of Federal Research in Support of High-Growth Businesses." It calls on all federal agencies to create plans for improving technology transfer of federally-funded research and development (R&D), at federal labs, and with universities, companies, and contract research organizations that receive federal support. The 131 universities we spoke with provided many insights about their relationship with federal agencies. Some of those ideas are referenced in this report. Over the next few years, federal agencies, under the leadership of the National Institute of Standards and Technology, will develop plans for greater commercialization of their research and development (R&D) efforts. This report is part of a larger effort by the federal government to improve its technology transfer activities and external partnerships, thus enabling more effective targeted federal support of university and college programs that promote innovation and commercialization.

INTRODUCTION

> "The key to our success...will be to compete by developing new products, by generating new industries, by maintaining our role as the world's engine of scientific discovery and technological innovation. It's absolutely essential to our future."[4]
>
> – President Barack Obama, November 17, 2010

America's innovative and entrepreneurial culture is often regarded as one of this country's greatest national advantages in an increasingly competitive world. This innovation infrastructure includes a large number of universities and colleges, research institutions, laboratories, and startup companies all across the United States - from major cities to rural areas. Every day, these institutions, often in partnership with federal agencies, develop breakthrough technologies in the life sciences, energy, telecommunications, information technology, education, social innovation, and other areas. This, in turn, has attracted many of the world's best and brightest people to pursue careers in R&D and innovation in the United States. Many of these same minds become leaders and entrepreneurs across the nation – creating cutting-edge innovation products and services and building our great companies.

As other nations increasingly compete with the United States for leadership in innovation,[5] America's colleges and universities are doing their part to maintain our leadership and to nurture more innovation, create processes and programs to commercialize that innovation, and promote

---

[4] See http://www.whitehouse.gov/the-press-office/2011/02/03/remarks-president-innovationpenn -state-university.

[5] U.S. Department of Commerce, "The Competitiveness and Innovative Capacity of the United States," January 2012. See http://www.commerce.gov/sites/default/files /documents/2012/january /competes_010511_0.pdf.

entrepreneurship as a viable career path for students. Universities use different approaches to encourage innovative thinking. Their approaches depend on their local environment and objectives, which in turn varies on geography, institutional size, history, culture, and funding resources. This diversity of approaches is proving to be both appropriate and successful for universities and colleges as they seek to create academic and economic benefits through innovation and entrepreneurship.

Across the United States, state and local governments, economic development agencies, non-profits, universities, and business groups are trying to develop innovation ecosystems that foster market-focused innovation and nurture startup companies to drive job creation. They all share some common goals - to find ways to create millions of new jobs in emerging industries where the United States can maintain its economic leadership, gain market share or create entirely new industries. At the same time, the challenges of globalization require that America remain nimble and constantly deliver new, innovative products and services. Research has shown that business startups and surviving young firms disproportionately create jobs relative to their size in the U.S. economy. For example, while firm startups only account for roughly three percent of total U.S. employment in any given year, they are responsible for about 20 percent of gross job creation.[6]

For the United States to remain economically competitive there is need for a strong national infrastructure to commercialize innovation and support high-growth entrepreneurship. If the nation needs to create millions of jobs, and many jobs are created by startup companies, then America will need to significantly increase the number of high-quality, startup companies in the coming years. In the United States, universities are a significant source of the ideas and R&D that are the value proposition of these high-growth startups. But those startups cannot be based solely in the traditional centers of American innovation, such as Silicon Valley, Boston, New York, and North Carolina. In order to develop local entrepreneurial ecosystems, these startups must also be based in new cities and rural communities in order to build their long-term economic prospects.

Unfortunately, the rate of startup formation has slowed over the past several years. According to a report from the McKinsey Global Institute (MGI), the United States could have created almost two million more jobs in 2010 if new business creation and employment at new businesses had

[6] Haltiwanger, John C., Ron S. Jarmin, and Javier Miranda, "Who Creates Jobs? Small vs. Large vs. Young," NBER Working Paper No. 16300, August 2010. See http://www.nber.org /papers/w16300.pdf?new_window=1

remained at the same pace as in 2007. Furthermore, the report stresses that returning to historic rates of startup formation will be key to achieving high future growth rates in employment.[7] Another MGI report also highlighted the importance of startup companies to economic growth, finding that around one third of the change in economic growth can be explained by changes in startup rates.[8] In other words, when economic growth increases, about one third of that growth can be attributed to increases in startup rates. These statistics, when factored in with research findings based on Census data,[9] validate the critical and growing role of the startup company in job creation and economic growth.

Fortunately, in many industries a combination of innovation and development of new business models has drastically reduced the cost of starting and building a company. Startups can launch and grow quickly without necessarily depending on large quantities of elusive venture capital. This change has been well documented and is facilitated by the emergence of cloud computing; the ability to find contract partners to manage administrative services, such as payroll, human resources, and accounting; the growth of micro-targeted "apps" for a wide variety of needs; the ability to use social media for targeted marketing; and access to inexpensive credit. Finally, the rise of "Do-It-Yourself" prototyping companies and affordable 3-D printers has led to a flourishing community of startup manufacturers that can leverage these tools to create and market products in a customized, but scalable, manner. These low-cost opportunities are being embraced effusively by college students as they "bootstrap" their businesses while remaining students.

Scattered throughout this report are examples of colleges and universities that are nurturing innovation and entrepreneurship in unique ways - from creating educational value and outlets for their students to providing new economic opportunities for their local economies.

We know of at least 450 colleges and universities across the United States now have entrepreneurship programs. Although universities are starting at

---

[7] Manyika, James, Susan Lund, Byron Auguste, Lenny Mendonca, Tim Welsh and Sreenivas Ramaswamy, "An Economy that Works: Job Creation and America's Future," McKinsey Global Institute, June 2011. See http:// www.mckinsey.com/insights/mgi /research/labor_ markets/an_economy_ that_works_ for_us_job_creation.

[8] McKinsey & Company, "The Power of Many: Realizing the Socioeconomic Potential of Entrepreneurs in the 21st Century Economy," G20 Young Entrepreneur Summit, October 2011. See http://www.mckinsey.com/locations/paris/home/The Power of Many- McKinsey Report- 20111005.pdf.

[9] U.S. Census Bureau, Business Dynamic Statistics (BDS). See http://www.census.gov/ces /dataproducts/bds/.

different places, their ability to mobilize their communities to become entrepreneurial is vital in creating a legion of high-growth startups. By engaging a broad yet diverse swath of the university community (students, faculty, alumni, local business and civic leaders) in entrepreneurship activities, universities and colleges aim to catalyze more solutions to major societal and economic problems–from inside and outside the lab–and to create an infrastructure supporting startup creation. Research universities in particular, are creating a culture of student and faculty entrepreneurship and seeking greater industry collaboration and commercialization of new technologies from their R&D efforts.

As the Office of Innovation and Entrepreneurship (OIE) at the U.S. Department of Commerce's Economic Development Administration talked to university leaders across the United States, they spoke about their growing roles in driving regional economic development. Universities are expanding beyond being primarily providers of innovation for their communities to also being a partner in vibrant local and regional ecosystems that include other universities, federal labs, startup companies, accelerators, and state and local organizations and improving access to public infrastructure. Many universities and colleges regard the model developed by the Massachusetts Institute of Technology (MIT) as a means of benchmarking their own roles in their communities.[10] MIT measures the economic value created by companies started by or affiliated with their alumni. In addition to creating tremendous economic value around the world, MIT found that nearly one-third of their entrepreneurs were not engineers, but from other disciplines, reflecting the broad-based nature of high growth innovation.

A McKinsey Global Institute (MGI) report on entrepreneurship indicated that there are three pillars to the platform that enables innovation and entrepreneurship to flourish, and universities are increasingly driving or involved in each of these factors: developing fertile innovation ecosystems, creating an entrepreneurial culture, and providing sustained financing for new ventures.[11] Foremost, creating an innovation ecosystem is critical for the long-term success and quality of entrepreneurial activity. It is important to have a strong local base for entrepreneurship that is supported by regional economic

[10] Roberts, Edward B. and Charles Eesley, "Entrepreneurial Impact: The Role of MIT," MIT Sloan School of Management, February 2009. See http://entrepreneurship.mit.edu /sites/default/files/files/Entrepreneurial_Impact_The_Role_of_MIT.pdf.

[11] McKinsey & Company, "The Power of Many: Realizing the Socioeconomic Potential of Entrepreneurs in the 21st Century Economy," G20 Young Entrepreneur Summit, October 2011. See http://www.mckinsey.com/locations/paris/home/The Power of Many- McKinsey Report- 20111005.pdf.

development plans. American colleges and universities often are the centerpiece of regional economic development strategies because they are often the main the source of innovation, but also train the local talent base and workforce, and can connect various actors to drive a common agenda. Secondly, they often push for cultural change on their campuses and within their communities, which sustains the innovation ecosystem. This includes everything from targeted entrepreneurship education to greater ties with local industry, such as licensing technologies locally.

The third factor suggested by the McKinsey report is the importance of available financing, in particular, early-stage and sustained financing. While colleges and universities traditionally have not provided financing for company startups, they have begun creating their own investment funds to support their home-grown entrepreneurs. Sometimes these funds are created through university endowments, specialized donations, or sponsorships. In addition, many university leaders have called upon the federal government to create funding and other assistance programs to fund the "valley of death" that innovative technologies face before their business model is clear. This has become very important to the major public research universities – many of whom are not based in major urban areas. According to data from the National Venture Capital Association, in the first half of 2012, almost three-quarters of venture capital investments in the United States were concentrated in three states – California, Massachusetts, and New York, and accounted for about 60 percent of all venture-backed deals. In the same time period, half of the states had only five or fewer venture-backed deals. This has led universities to step in and fill the void themselves and ask for federal support.

A recent report by the National Research Council, "Rising to the Challenge: U.S. Innovation Policy for the Global Economy," highlights the importance of university linkages to the market to better promote university-based innovation and entrepreneurship.[12] The report reflects, and encourages the idea of universities developing their own entrepreneurial infrastructure through four support strategies:

The creation of matching funds to a fund that is set aside by universities to nurture innovation and entrepreneurship;

The creation and support of accelerators on campus or affiliated with universities to help spinoffs grow without losing their connection to local innovation;

[12] National Research Council, "Rising to the Challenge: U.S. Innovation Policy for the Global Economy," The National Academies Press, Washington, DC. 2012. See www.nap.edu.

The creation of funding mechanisms to help with commercialization and overcoming the "Valley of Death;" and

Helping universities and colleges learn from each other and stay aware of best practices, emerging trends and new ideas.

OIE began a series of discussions with the leadership of major research universities, regional state universities, community colleges, Historically Black Colleges and Universities (HBCU), and federal research labs to understand the diversity of approaches to innovation, commercialization, and entrepreneurship that they have undertaken. Initially, this outreach was conducted as follow up to a letter addressed to the U.S. Secretary of Commerce that was submitted by 141 university presidents, chancellors, and higher education association leaders through the National Advisory Council on Innovation and Entrepreneurship (NACIE). This letter identified five areas where universities were supporting innovation and entrepreneurship. Those categories included:

Promoting student innovation and entrepreneurship,
Encouraging faculty innovation and entrepreneurship,
Actively supporting university technology transfer,
Facilitating university-industry collaboration, and
Engaging in regional and local economic development efforts.

These five categories reflect the widespread importance of innovation and entrepreneurship to the mission and activities of higher education. OIE found that universities do not view innovation and entrepreneurship as a short-term revenue opportunity, but as a long-term investment in their students, faculty, alumni, supporters, and communities.

Student entrepreneurship serves as a critical gateway for universities to comprehensively embrace innovation and entrepreneurship. While many universities may hope that their students are secretly working on the next Apple® or Google®, their main objective is to provide educational value in a way that will focus students' energies to help them identify and embrace their areas of interest, and supplement their classroom education with the development of life skills, such as budgeting, marketing, and professionalism. Many universities believe that they will benefit more through sustained relationships with their graduates, rather than by acquiring financial equity from student startups.

Faculty entrepreneurship policies are designed to connect research to market and societal relevance and to find solutions to real-world problems.

Universities are encouraging faculty entrepreneurship by creating flexible work place policies, financial awards, and making seed funding available to faculty, researchers, and graduate students, as tools for retention, revenue, income supplementation, and as a way to keep faculty motivated and engaged. It is also a reflection of a larger desire among a new generation of faculty to be more relevant to the world around them.

The traditional home for starting the commercialization of university-based innovation and entrepreneurship is the university's technology transfer office (TTO). In recent years, and despite criticism, the TTO continues to be the hub and engine of the commercialization process on campuses. TTOs are however taking on a greater role than merely assisting with patenting and introducing faculty and students to investors. TTOs are organizing networks across the universities' communities, growing their teams in order to better understand new technologies, and organizing programming across campus departments. TTOs also are aligning their goals with university advancement, and are developing shared strategies around fundraising, alumni engagement and corporate relations.

The need to collaborate with industry has grown in importance as access to federal funding declines. Not only are universities licensing inventions to, and collaborating with, established companies, but they are also increasing their support for home-grown startup companies. They continue, though, to recognize that larger, established companies remain an important source of revenue. Universities remain keenly aware of the importance of the private sector to their mission, because private industry will ultimately house both their innovations and students when they leave the university. In addition to licensing innovation and hiring their students, private industry is actually a producer of innovation itself, and has a much deeper understanding of the broader business climate and models to commercialize any given invention.

Finally, universities are looking at innovation, commercialization, and entrepreneurship as part of their role in the economic development of their local economies – at the local and state levels. While universities have always had an important role in their communities, the points of engagement are rapidly changing. Instead of focusing solely on the economic impact of their graduate hires or of the physical expansion of university facilities, universities are establishing programs to engage their globally competitive talent to develop local and regional economies— the engine of job creation and economic growth in the United States.

The NACIE-sponsored university presidents' letter was just one of several efforts by higher education institutions focused on innovation and entrepreneurship. As part of the Startup America Initiative,[13] the National Association of Community College Entrepreneurship (NACCE) also enlisted 170 community college presidents to commit to entrepreneurship programs on their campuses. The HBCU community, through the work of the United Negro College Fund and the HBCU Business School Deans, is reaching out to its schools to help launch entrepreneurship and social entrepreneurship programs. Regional state colleges also began entrepreneurship programs as a means of keeping their graduates in their local areas. These efforts have many of the same characteristics as those of the NACIE-letter signatories, with a focus on idea generation, business model and leadership development, and local and regional development. This report seeks to highlight this alignment and assist colleges and universities that are striving to expand innovation and entrepreneurship opportunities.

The NACIE-sponsored university presidents' letter identified multiple areas where the federal government could engage the university community.

First, it became clear in conversations with university and business leaders that federal agencies will need to adapt to emerging technologies and ideas in two very important ways. Today's innovation is multi-disciplinary in nature – across geographies, specialties, and fields. Wireless health is an example of a complex technology that merges the functionality of wireless technology, information technology, medical devices, and biotechnology – areas that are not currently within the purview of a single federal agency. The development of such a multi-disciplinary technology changes the relationships between federal agencies and their interactions with the university and business communities. The Economic Development Administration's (EDA) i6 Challenge and Jobs and Innovation Accelerator Challenges,[14,15] and the National Science Foundation's I-Corps,[16] are attempts to address this emerging issue, with multiple agencies pooling their funding for targeted support in multi-disciplinary areas such as advanced manufacturing or proof of concept development.

Second, those organizations that seek to better support high-growth innovation and entrepreneurship, from government agencies to non-profits and accelerators, must be able to understand the needs of high-growth startups and their emerging technologies. Universities are recruiting outside partners to better train their students and faculty on the strategic needs of innovation-

[13] See http://www.whitehouse.gov/startup-america-fact-sheet.
[14] See http://www.eda.gov/challenges/i6/.
[15] See http://www.eda.gov/challenges/jobsaccelerator/.
[16] See http://www.nsf.gov/news/special_reports/i-corps/.

driven, high growth companies. University and business leaders see these areas of integration as critical to the success of those startups, and in helping the United States in areas of strategic national importance, such as manufacturing, exports, and investment.

The "Innovative and Entrepreneurial University" is a combination of the most innovative, interesting, and successful examples of what universities and colleges are doing around the country to foster innovation and entrepreneurship. This report will leave the reader optimistic about America's leadership in innovation and the ability of our entrepreneurs to grow our economy and create high-quality jobs. America's universities and colleges are indeed on the move. Whether just getting started with entrepreneurship clubs or raising multi-million dollar gifts to scale up their commercialization efforts, the nation's colleges and universities have elevated the topics of innovation and entrepreneurship to national prominence. The hope is that this report will spark the generation of even more ideas and discussions in higher education that will continue to move these topics forward.

I. PROMOTING STUDENT INNOVATION AND ENTREPRENEURSHIP

The main priority of any university and college system is education. Many universities are expanding their educational curricula and programs to foster innovation and entrepreneurship. Universities increasingly offer courses and programs in entrepreneurship and related fields for undergraduate, graduate, and postdoctoral students. Students develop a better understanding of innovation and entrepreneurship, through newly-established curricula, minors, majors, and certificate programs that cut across educational disciplines, and through educational programs that emphasize hands-on learning. Many universities are also augmenting traditional classroom instruction in novel ways. Universities are increasing educational opportunities outside of the classroom to include student housing and dormitories that directly foster the entrepreneurial spirit. Student clubs, centered on multi-dimensional entrepreneurship activities, also are on the rise. Most campuses run a variety of business plan and venture competitions that offer students support networks, such as mentors and training opportunities, to help them further develop their innovative ideas.

Courses and Degree Programs in Innovation and Entrepreneurship

Many universities are seeing an increase in student demand for innovation and entrepreneurship, broadening course and program offerings. Entrepreneurship courses and programs equip students with a wide range of valuable skills, including business-plan development, marketing, networking, creating "elevator pitches," attracting financing (such as seed capital), and connecting with local business leaders. Some universities are offering bachelor and master's degree programs and concentrations in innovation and entrepreneurship, expanding upon traditional Bachelor of Arts (B.A.) and Bachelor of Science (B.S.) degrees (Box 1.1). Many business schools are breaking down traditional barriers and encouraging entrepreneurship through multi-disciplinary courses and programs to students of all academic disciplines.

Box 1.1. The University of Colorado's Innovation and Entrepreneur Degree Program

Located at the Colorado Springs campus, this program offers a Bachelor's degree in Innovation (B.I.), which provides a unique multi-disciplinary team approach. For example, in addition to completing classes in computer science, a B.I. in Computer Science requires students to develop strong team skills, study innovation, engage in entrepreneurship, practice proposal writing, and learn business and intellectual property law.

Accreditation remains an important issue to the academic community. While many schools now offer entrepreneurship courses, many commented about the inability to develop certificates, programs, and degrees without proper guidance and standards for entrepreneurship education. Many anticipate that in the coming years the leading accreditation agencies, along with state education agencies, and the U.S. Departments of Labor and Education, will come together to address this issue, and that this will eventually lead to a great expansion of formal programs in this space.

Experiential Learning

Experiential or applied learning has been increasing in popularity at universities and colleges for many years now. This type of education improves upon traditional classroom instruction—which consists mainly of lectures and fact-based memorization—by actively engaging students in innovative and entrepreneurial activities through workshops, conferences, internships, hands-on experience, and real-world projects (Box 1.2). Experiential learning in innovation and entrepreneurship has spread outside of business schools and moved into the fine arts, science, and engineering programs. Universities and colleges also support specialized internship programs focused on entrepreneurship education and technology innovation that match students directly to start-up projects, technology transfer offices, venture capital firms, and industry. This variety of educational opportunities allows students to address real-world challenges in a supportive educational environment.

Box 1.2. Examples of Experiential Learning Opportunities

University of Illinois' Patent Clinic provides law students the opportunity to draft patent applications for student inventors. Student-innovators with potentially patentable inventions are referred to the Patent Clinic by the Technology Entrepreneur Center (TEC) at the College of Engineering. The Patent Clinic then reviews the innovations, searches for relevant prior art, and selects one innovation for each law student. Each law student then proceeds to work with the inventors to draft a patent application on their innovation in consultation with an instructor.

The University of Wisconsin-Madison's "Entrepreneurial Deli" borrows a food court metaphor to help students meet and learn from experienced young entrepreneurs. Using the tag line "Grab 'n Go Entrepreneurship" and a speed-dating-like format, the workshops encourage students to learn first-hand about solutions to different problems that confront startup ventures from experienced entrepreneurs.

Washington University in St. Louis' student internship program offers 25 paid internships per summer for students to work in a start-up company four days a week and attend experience learning workshops one day a week.

The University of California at San Diego's Rady School of Business requires its management students to take a course entitled "lab to market."

In Lab to Market, MBAs create new products or services and go through the commercialization process, with advice from faculty and business mentors.

Competitive Opportunities

Competitions are an excellent way to actively engage faculty and students in the learning process. As a whole, business plan competitions are geared toward teaching students how to think outside the classroom, fostering collaborations across disciplines and increasing access to businesses. Competitions provide an exciting platform for students to learn practical skills, such as how to craft a business plan, access venture funding, and pitch ideas. Sequential competitions build upon project ideas, ultimately leading to completed business plans that are ready for possible funding from investors. Universities understand this, and are transitioning away from single monetary rewards for competitions and are increasingly recognizing milestone achievements with a multitude of prizes, including non-monetary resources such as incubator space and mentorships (Box 1.3). Some universities are expanding their student team competitions to include faculty and alumni, and increasing the scope and size of the pool of resources through collaboration with industry and local partners.

Box 1.3. Examples of Business Plan Competitions

Rice University makes over $1.2 million available in cash, prizes, and in-kind resources to winners to provide seed funding to launch companies. These funds serve as seed funding for many of the winning teams.

Florida Atlantic University (FAU) provides the winner of their business plan competition with free space in the incubator for half a year.

Michigan Technology University's business plan competition winners are rewarded with a monetary prize that goes directly to their business, instead of to the individual. The following year, the winners will highlight their business milestones that have resulted from the funding.

University of Washington has a stage-gated business plan competition comprised of different competitions throughout the school year in combination with seminars, courses, and mentorship to assist in advancing student ideas to the next level.

The competitions range across disciplines and industries, bringing students together from different departments.

University of Oregon's Venture Launch Pathway program, student teams pick from technologies from many sources included federal labs, companies, universities and technologies from other countries. The technologies that look most promising are advanced by student teams, with backgrounds in law, business, and sciences, into the international business competition circuit.

The University of Wisconsin has a 100 hour challenge in which students must purchase a product, change it, and create a public URL for outreach. They are then tested on many different aspects of entrepreneurship.

University of Louisiana—Lafayette hosts the Innov8 Lafayette program. This eight day, community-wide program includes specific activities centered on the importance of innovation. Some activities are focused on the environment, entrepreneurship, and the arts.

When discussing the role of federal agencies in this space, many universities commented on two recent actions by the Obama Administration. First, on the possible expansion of an innovative program launched by the U.S. Department of Energy in 2012. This National Business Plan contest[17] provided seed funding and technical support to regional business plan contests at universities and in communities. The program connected the Department of Energy with a large group of leading entrepreneurs and innovators in the energy space for a relatively small amount of sponsorship. Many universities hoped that other agencies would also look at this model as a way to access market intelligence, cutting-edge technology solutions, and as a way to engage better with entrepreneurs and startups.

In addition, many universities are hopeful that recent guidance provided by the U.S. Department of Treasury about Program Related Investments (PRI),[18] could greatly increase the amount of philanthropic investment in their student entrepreneurs. The guidance put forth by Treasury makes it easier for philanthropic entities, such as foundations and trusts, to directly invest in for-

[17] U.S. Department of Energy, National Clean Energy Business Plan Competition. See http://techportal.eere.energy.gov/commercialization/ natlbizplan.html.

[18] U.S. Department of the Treasury, proposed regulations for program-related investments by private foundations. See http://www.irs.gov/Charities-&-Non-Profits/Examples-of-Program-Related-Investments-by-Private-Foundations-%E2%80%93-Proposed-Regulations.

profit entities that share their mission. This will greatly expand access to philanthropic funds, in addition to traditional investor capital, to advance socially beneficial technologies in food, energy, and health.

Entrepreneurial and Innovation Collaboration Spaces

Entrepreneurial and innovation "living spaces" are a unique trend in motivating student involvement outside the classroom setting. These spaces use the power of proximity to promote student engagement in developing innovative ideas and starting businesses (Box 1.4). Some universities are embracing the entrepreneurial dorm, whereas others are expanding this concept to promote entrepreneurial clusters, within the university and sometimes stretching into local communities. Entrepreneurial spaces facilitate student access to learning and networking opportunities with local entrepreneurs and innovators. These spaces also host a variety of student entrepreneur clubs that serve as a premier resource for aspiring student entrepreneurs and foster a community of like-minded peers. These clubs are geared toward building financial literacy and leadership skills, as well as encouraging students to pursue commercialization opportunities for innovative ideas and technologies.

Box 1.4. Examples of Living and Learning Spaces

University of Florida's Inspiration Hall is a new, state-of-the-art live-and-learn community located within Innovation Square, only two blocks from the University of Florida and the Florida Innovation Hub. By living and learning within the Innovation Square environment, undergraduate students can interact throughout their academic program with other like-minded people: fellow students, researchers, faculty, business professionals and entrepreneurs.

Purdue University has an Entrepreneurship and Innovation Learning Community (ELC) that is made up of students interested in new business ventures that live together in Harrison Hall, many of whom also participate in the entrepreneurship certificate program.

Community College Entrepreneurship

As part of the Startup America Initiative, 170 community colleges across the United States have launched entrepreneurship programs. These programs are often taking the same shape as those at larger research universities. Institutions such as Lorain Community College OH offers incubators and shared facilities for their students and regional entrepreneurs while Middlesex Community College, MA, provides seed funding for their students to launch entrepreneurial ventures. Community colleges are embracing entrepreneurship for the same reasons as their colleagues in research universities. It reflects their student desires, the changing nature of their local economies, and a change in their role in workforce training with larger companies. Many of them have expressed the desire to see entrepreneurship become a career pathway for their students similar to other career fields.

II. ENCOURAGING FACULTY INNOVATION AND ENTREPRENEURSHIP

A new generation of faculty on America's campuses is striving to conduct world-class research, while working to identify the relevance of their research for solving real-world problems. To address this issue, these institutions are fostering faculty entrepreneurship through educational opportunities, acknowledging technology development, increasing transfer and commercialization achievements, and facilitating collaborative efforts. This commitment to promoting innovation pushes faculty to identify and employ available networks and resources to pursue innovation and entrepreneurship opportunities. New faculty orientations, boot-camps, and seminar events focusing on innovation and entrepreneurship are examples of some of the educational opportunities offered to faculty. Campuses are actively connecting faculty to networks of recognized entrepreneurs and industry partners, to promote cross-disciplinary efforts. Faculty tenure considerations and other rewards are on the raise, incorporating faculty contributions in innovation and technology transfer efforts, while providing the incentives to engage in R&D, technology development, and business start-up efforts.

The Changing Innovation Culture

On trend is a shift in the hiring and retention culture across many universities. Today, institutions hire faculty who are interested not only in the advancement of their academic areas but also in pursuing commercial applications for their technologies, or engage in entrepreneurial activities that correlate with their academic disciplines. New faculty orientations often include workshops and training to help faculty navigate technology transfer offices and find the resources available to them on campus. Universities also offer faculty training in areas such as professional mentoring, prototype development, business planning, and market testing (Box 2.1). An evolving university innovation culture provides faculty with the essential information and incentives to move from a narrowly-focused scientific research tradition to a more forward-looking, comprehensive innovative process that incorporates technology development and commercialization efforts.

Box 2.1. The University of Pittsburgh Offers a Business of Innovation Commercialization Course

The Office of Technology Management and the Office of the Provost hosts an annual, seven-week course aimed at educating and motivating both student and faculty researchers in innovation development, commercialization, and entrepreneurship. The course takes participants through each step of the innovation and commercialization process, from idea conception to intellectual property protection and licensing, and all the way to early-stage market research and networking strategies. Private, individualized workshops are also offered where students can explore their own innovation ideas in a team setting.

Rewarding Faculty Innovation and Entrepreneurship

Universities and colleges are celebrating faculty achievements in innovation and entrepreneurship. These acknowledgments include campus-wide prizes and award ceremonies that bring the faculty community together to recognize and learn about the accomplishments of their peers across academic disciplines (Box 2.2). Awards such as "Innovator of the Year" and "Faculty Entrepreneur of the Year" are popular as they reward faculty for achievements that reach beyond traditional research and teaching accomplishments. Universities and colleges are updating tenure and sabbatical leave guidelines to encourage faculty to pursue collaborative and entrepreneurial endeavors, such as launching a start-up company (Box 2.3). Some programs allow faculty time off to engage in innovation and entrepreneurial activities, without incurring any penalty towards tenure and promotion. Providing leave to pursue entrepreneurial activities increases the potential for the successful technology development and commercialization of research, while adding to faculty's understanding of the commercialization process, enabling them to incorporate new material into student instruction. This flexibility also improves the focus of R&D efforts and facilitates public engagement by encouraging faculty to commercialize their research.

Box 2.2. University of Southern California

The university promotes faculty entrepreneurship and innovation by supporting, rewarding, and funding the work of faculty members. The Lloyd Greif Center for Entrepreneurial Studies presents three faculty members with research grants totaling $11,000 as part of annual Faculty Research Awards. The Center also rewards entrepreneurial-minded faculty with the annual Greif Research Impact Award, which is given to the faculty member who has written an article that has the most effect on the area of entrepreneurship.

Box 2.3. University of Virginia

In 2010, UVA's School of Medicine was among the first to include innovation and entrepreneurship activities among its promotion and tenure criteria. Candidates for promotion and tenure are asked to provide a report on their inventions and the patent status of those inventions; registered copyright materials; license agreements involving their technologies; and any other contributions to technology transfer-related activities, including entrepreneurship and economic development impact.

Finding the appropriate rewards and policies to promote faculty innovation is complex. Internal policies for faculty innovation performance usually are evaluated at the discretion of individual departments. For these programs to be successful in spurring innovation out of the higher educational system, universities and colleges need increased flexibility in developing faculty tenure, leave regulations, and other faculty-based policies that facilitate innovation and entrepreneurship.

Supporting Collaboration

As faculty become more interested in commercialization activities, universities are providing additional resources to encourage collaboration with local communities and industries. A few universities have hired individuals, or created teams, to connect faculty with similar interests and research goals—often reaching across academic departments—to share information and experience on creating startups, licensing technology, and collaborating with industry. This cross-disciplinary effort helps share information on best practices and spurs new ideas for developing and commercializing new products.

Universities and colleges are also inviting community leaders and local entrepreneurs to become more involved in the development of technology and startup companies (Box 2.4). A few universities have developed programs to link experienced entrepreneurs with faculty to assist in the startup process, development, and longevity. In most cases, faculty returns to teach and continue research, allowing the non-university collaborative partners to take over the leadership role and continue to develop and expand the companies. Entrepreneurs also serve in a mentoring role, helping faculty to identify and further develop commercialization opportunities.

Box 2.4. The University of Cincinnati Research Institute (UCRI)

The University's non-profit allows local, national, and international industries to partner with expert faculty and students performing sponsored research. These partnerships not only connect university experts with industry, but also facilitate the commercialization of research, and enhance cooperative and experiential learning experiences and opportunities. With the creation of the foundation outside the university, professors and other state employees remain in compliance with state restrictions on equity and revenues streams, while allowing them to be compensated for their work through income from licensing revenues and other shares.

To capitalize on the expertise of seasoned entrepreneurs, many universities are building entrepreneurin-residence (EIR) programs. The EIRs work with university researchers, students, faculty, and staff in the development of early stage start-up companies to provide guidance and advice. EIRs help interested faculty members better understand entrepreneurship, evaluate technology for licensing, expand their network of resources, and guide them on how to start the commercialization process (Box 2.5). EIRs usually have a focus area that meets faculty needs, often have a good working knowledge of current intellectual property laws and can assist faculty in finding those ideas in their research programs that are worth commercializing. The EIR program provides mentorship opportunities that help stimulate innovative and entrepreneurial activity throughout campus.

Box 2.5. University of Nebraska Medical Center – Entrepreneur in Residence

The EIR works with licensing staff and researchers at the University of Nebraska Medical Center to help identify, evaluate, develop, and support the creation of business plans and new companies based on technology developed at UNMC. The EIR is an industry expert with scientific, entrepreneurial, managerial, and financial experience who works side by side with UNMC scientists to identify, evaluate, and support the development of new start-up companies based on technology license agreements from UNeMed.

Engaging with Industry

Faculty is increasing its engagement with industry to obtain research and technology development ideas, capital, and other types of support. Many universities host events to bring faculty, industry, angel investors, and venture capitalists together for networking opportunities (Box 2.6). These events give industry an early look at R&D activities on campus, while providing faculty with networking and funding possibilities. Examples of such events include lunch-and-learn series, rapid-fire networking programs, seminars, and workshops.

Box 2.6. California Institute of Technology

The university runs a comprehensive "tech review" process for faculty, in which Caltech researchers have the opportunity to give a short presentation on a new and promising technology for commercialization to an audience of angel investors, venture capitalists, and entrepreneurial alumni. A roundtable discussion then takes place where investors provide feedback and advice on commercial development potential of the technology.

A common theme developing across campuses large and small is the importance of creating connections between faculty and the outside world. Programs, such as proof-of-concept, are meant to connect faculty research topics to market relevance, while externships and leave of absence policies are designed to provide faculty with the time they need to understand the latest trends and technologies in industry in their fields of science. Although the NACIE-led letter prioritized these sorts of programs, they have not grown as quickly as expected due to a combination of budgetary issues and faculty interests.

As universities provide faculty with increased educational opportunities, celebrate their innovative achievements, and enable collaboration with experienced entrepreneurs and business communities, an entrepreneurial culture is developed throughout the educational system. Students also can benefit from the on-going education and experiences of faculty. Through dedicated institutional support, faculties across academic disciplines are able to work together with each other, community entrepreneurs, and businesses to develop new technology and create start-up companies.

III. Actively Supporting Technology Transfer

Effectively transforming research and ideas into marketable products and services is often a lengthy and complex process requiring substantial resources. The university and college systems are one of the most important sources of the nation's R&D output. The goal of a Technology Transfer Office (TTO) at a college or university is to protect and promote the research developed by its faculty and students through commercialization and patents. Once the research is protected, the technology and information can be released, providing social and economic benefits.

Reducing Technology Transfer Barriers

A high priority for the nation's university and college system is to streamline the technology transfer process, to more effectively identify research with market potential, and to move it from the lab to the marketplace. Universities are broadening their technology transfer functions to meet the growing demand of their services while working to minimize the costs and risks of commercializing research. They are accomplishing this by expanding TTO facilities, hiring skilled staff, improving technical support to researchers, and increasing access to capital for researchers.

The success of these heightened technology transfer efforts at universities is evident by an increase in licensing and startup activity.[19] According to a licensing survey by the Association of University Technology Managers (AUTM), the number of licenses executed in fiscal year (FY) 2011 rose 14 percent compared to FY 2010, and the number of startups formed was up three percent during the same time period.

Reducing these barriers while also developing common standards is critical to the TTOs seeking to add societal benefit and impact to their missions. As entrepreneurs today move towards a greater focus on the triple bottom line (environmental, social, and economic or "planet, people, and profit"), TTOs are increasingly being asked about their processes for patenting low-cost and environmentally-friendly innovations as well as those innovations that investors may be interested in funding using microfinance models. Consequently, TTOs are developing processes for these sectors to integrate into the model of their traditional work.

Expanding TTOs Level of Support

TTOs are hiring more skilled professional staff with experience in areas such as intellectual property law, licensing, and in developing and managing university-industry partnerships. In addition, a university's TTO often taps into institutional resources such as law and business graduate students and faculty. Examples of other skills sought by TTOs include marketing, accounting, and regulatory compliance (Box 3.1). Acquiring experienced staff and in-house assistance not only leverages internal resources but also reduces

---

[19] Association of University Technology Managers, "AUTM U.S. Licensing Activity Survey: Highlights," See http://www.autm.net/AM/Template.cfm?Section= FY_2011_ Licensing_ Activity_Survey&Template=/CM/ContentDisplay.cfm&ContentID=8731

the costs and time associated with filing patent applications and negotiating technology licenses. TTOs are also integrating accomplished entrepreneurs to consult with students and faculty about building startup companies to foster their technologies.

An emerging trend in technology transfer is the establishment of "one-stop-shops" that provide assistance, mentorship, and information on patenting and licensing processes to faculty and student inventors. These "shops" streamline the technology disclosure process and integrate all technology transfer functions into one facility. Interested faculty and students can explore the start-up potential for their inventions and can obtain assistance during the technology development and marketing. TTOs are also expanding beyond their traditional areas of focus, namely the hard sciences and engineering. Today, many TTOs provide guidance in navigating licensing processes and commercialization opportunities for innovative work in areas such as education, criminology, organizational structure, music, dance, and the fine arts. NACIE's letter to the Secretary of Commerce recommended the importance of building a common platform to connect similar efforts – so that institutions know what research, intellectual property development, and programming their peers are involved with.

Box 3.1. Utah State University

The university's Intellectual Property (IP) Services unit within Commercial Enterprises helps USU faculty and staff manage and protect intellectual property. IP service managers work and assist USU and USURF researchers to identify, disclose, protect, and commercialize USU intellectual property. IP Services includes two IP attorneys, one registered patent agent, one paralegal and one docket manager.

The fastest growing trend in this space is the rise of Proof of Concept Centers, such as the MIT Deshpande Center for Technological Innovation and the Von Liebig Center at the University of California San Diego. These centers have a variety of programs that collectively achieve three goals: increase the volume and diversity of entrepreneurship on campus, improve the quality of startups and entrepreneurs on campus, and be increasingly engaged with local investors and entrepreneurs so that the university's startups stay local.

Box 3.2. University of Toledo

The "Lab-to-Launch" initiative partners UT's technology transfer team with Rocket Ventures LLC, a pre-seed fund, to accelerate the transfer of research to the market. The team works closely with research faculty to identify and promote high-potential platform technologies and expedite the transfer of university research into commercial products and services, with particular emphasis on regional economic development.

TTOs are also hiring undergraduate and graduate students both as interns and employees (Box 3.3). These students acquire experience working on commercialization projects and the associated challenges, such as the patenting and licensing process, and to how access funding. Some students sort through faculty R&D submissions and help identify university research with technical viability and commercial value. Other students, in particular law and business school students, help file patent applications, share information on intellectual property rights, consult on internal strategy, and provide business development coaching. A few TTOs offer lecture series to faculty and students on technology transfer topics to attract more interest and educate on commercial viability.

Box 3.3. Examples of Educational Hands on Learning and Workshops

University of North Carolina Chapel Hill's Office of Technology Development (OTD) internship program is an eight-month position for graduate students or post-doctoral fellows who wish to learn more about intellectual property protection and technology commercialization. The internship runs during the academic year and requires 8 to 12 hours a week, during which the interns participate in a formal training series covering the basics of technology transfer, market assessments, and direct marketing for select technologies. Interns also gain exposure to ongoing negotiations between the OTD and industry partners.

University of Rochester's F.I.R.E. Series is a regular lecture series designed to educate the university community about the many aspects of technology transfer, what it means to be an inventor, what every researcher should know in order to protect potential intellectual property rights, and the complexities of starting a business. This lecture series is run out of the University of Rochester Medical Center Office of Technology Transfer.

Cornell University IP&Pizza TM and IP&Pasta TM host outreach activities to Cornell faculty, research staff, and students. The goal of these activities is to increase appreciation of the importance of making university research results useful to society, providing a basic knowledge and understanding of intellectual property issues, and creating an awareness of capturing and protecting valuable intellectual property and its importance to entice potential industry partners. This and other similar programs are run through Cornell's Center for Technology and Enterprise and Commercialization.

Protecting Intellectual Property

Universities have created a variety of strategies to protect their intellectual property, which has raised the demand for intellectual property services and staff with knowledge of intellectual property laws and procedures. One reason for the increased demand is that many TTOs are now connecting with faculty early in the R&D process to encourage them to file patent applications prior to publicly releasing their results. One institution files a provisional patent application for every invention disclosure submitted by university researchers, while others are more selective and file a combination of provisional and utility (or regular) patent applications on technologies that appear to have the greatest licensing potential (Box 3.4). To provide faculty, students, and staff with incentives to protect intellectual property and pursue commercialization of research, universities are increasingly rewarding them by offering a greater share of licensing royalties and other commercialization income.

Box 3.4. California Institute of Technology

Caltech files a provisional patent application for every single invention disclosure that goes through their TTO. Over the first year following the filing of the provisional patent application, the TTO evaluates the technical and business merits of the invention to determine whether it is worth filing a regular patent application on the invention.

Shrinking the Funding Gap

Universities are working with their TTOs to provide and increase access to funding opportunities in order to help bridge the transition between research and technology development, commonly referred to as the "Valley of Death" (Box 3.5). Universities use a variety of funding mechanisms to bridge the Valley of Death. Many universities have created venture-, proof-of-concept-, and growth-funds to assist in the development of technology and startups resulting from university research. Additionally, universities have sought local community and alumni support to help TTOs meet the growing demand for venture funds and grants for seed funding. Convertible debt loans are used by some universities to ease commercialization, with faculty paying back a predetermined percent of start-up costs.

Box 3.5. Bridging the Funding Gap

University of Wisconsin's Wisconsin Alumni Research Foundation (WARF) is a nonprofit organization that started as a funding center from alumni contributions.

Today, WARF raises funds through licensing university research and technologies to companies for commercialization. The funds generated are used to fund research, build facilities, purchase equipment, and support faculty and student fellowships.

University of Oklahoma's Growth Fund provides money to researchers on each OU campus to help them develop prototypes and conduct additional research to keep research programs viable through the Valley of Death.

Temple University's Office of Technology Development and Commercialization has provided more than $130 million in funding to support advanced research commercialization at the university.

University of Colorado System's TTO Proof of Concept (POC) programs are supported by income generated from the commercialization of CU intellectual property. The CU TTO has created, and supports, POC funding opportunities for university research and business development. To date, TTO's POC programs have involved over 110 projects and more than $13 million in total funding.

University of Michigan's Gap Fund program was developed from the proceeds of the UM Tech Transfer central administration revenues, with matched funding from the State.

University of Minnesota's Internal Business Units (IBUs) program has developed an incubator space to help mature and launch early-stage technologies. IBUs address a small number of technologies that are nearly market ready but need some limited investment and early sales in order to be more attractive as startup opportunities. IBUs are an effective way to incubate those technologies in a business setting where they receive support from the university through seed funding and resources. IBUs are not a mechanism for bridging a broad "valley of death," or incubating technologies that will require a long period of development or significant seed funding, but rather represent an innovative strategy for new company development.

Emory University's Drug Innovation at Emory (DRIVE) is a non-profit drug development company separate from, but wholly owned by, the university.

DRIVE expands the capabilities of traditional academic drug discovery by combining the expertise of Emory scientists with industry drug development experts.

University of Akron's Akron Regional Change Angel (ARCHAngel) Network is a regional forum for introducing investors to market-driven, technology-based investment opportunities. It brings together promising technology companies and angel investors with a particular focus on businesses that leverage the region's strengths in healthcare, information technologies, polymers, and other advanced materials.

Regional Technology Transfer Centers

In various parts of the country, universities and non-profit research centers are already coming together to collaborate on the commercialization of research. According to a recent survey of its member's by the Association of Public Land Grant Universities (APLU), a large percentage of major public universities do not have separate technology transfer offices. In addition, students and alumni from smaller colleges often don't have an on-campus technology transfer office, and need support from others in their regions. Regional tech transfer centers are filling that role, by providing the technology transfer function across large universities, regional state universities, non-profit research organizations and small colleges across a region (Box 3.6). Universities such as the University of Utah and Texas System have taken the lead in developing these centers in order to collaborate better with their regional partners.

Box 3.6. University of Texas South Texas Technology Management Center

South Texas Technology Management (STTM) is a regional technology transfer office affiliated with the University of Texas Health Science Center at San Antonio (UTHSCSA), and has collaborated with the research departments of the University of Texas San Antonio (UTSA), the University of Texas Pan American (UTPA), Texas State University (TXState), the University of Texas at Brownsville (UTB) and Stephen F. Austin University (SFA). It provides a host of services for regional institutions such as support on grant applications, patenting, and commercialization.

Through the collaborative efforts STTM has built a portfolio of technologies and projects to take to push ideas to the next level. The Horizon fund provides $10 million to spin off companies created using University of Texas technology.

Several universities indicated that they experienced funding challenges in this area. In particular, there are very few sources of funding for innovation infrastructure – i.e., support for the organizations that bring together researchers, entrepreneurs, investors, and professional services to help deliver ideas to the marketplace. Often, private philanthropy and corporate sponsors are not interested in broad-based infrastructure support, but rather on programmatic funding for specific sectors. To help fill this void, the federal government has created grant challenge such as EDA's i6 Challenge and NSF's Innovation Corps, to provide flexible funding to support innovation infrastructure.

Presidential Memorandum on Accelerating Technology Transfer and Commercialization of Federal Research

In 2011, President Obama posted a Presidential Memorandum entitled "Accelerating Technology Transfer and Commercialization of Federal Research in Support of High-Growth Businesses." This Memorandum requires federal agencies highly involved in R&D and entrepreneurship to develop plans to greatly increase the commercialization of federally-funded R&D over the next several years. There are several proposed programs to guide technology transfer efforts in the federal government, but many of the agency decisions will also have an impact on universities.

The Interagency Working Group on Technology Transfer, managed by the National Institutes for Standards and Technology, has released its preliminary report on the implementation of the Presidential Memorandum. The various agency reports outline the unique programs and emerging best practices among federal agencies for partnering with outside R&D organizations such as universities and private industry, funding the commercialization of research, and assisting startup companies. In addition, federal agencies will put into place more robust metrics to measure the success of technology transfer and commercialization of federally-supported R&D. These metrics will help federal agencies identify the commercial impact of their in-house R&D, as well as that done with partners, such as universities.

IV. Facilitating University-Industry Collaboration

University-industry partnerships are essential for further developing ideas and technologies derived from university research. These partnerships are crucial for directing investment toward commercially promising research, and helping to bridge funding gaps that often exist at the technology development and marketing stages. Universities and industry have found that working together is mutually beneficial because knowledge and resources are shared to achieve common goals. Industry benefits from greater and earlier access to scientific expertise, intellectual property, and commercial opportunities, while universities benefit from enhanced educational opportunities for faculty and students, revenues from successful licensing agreements and ventures, and local and regional development.

Sharing Resources and Knowledge

As federal resources become limited, universities are seeking broader channels of support for technology development and commercialization efforts, particularly from the business community. Several universities are creating "front-door policies" to easily engage private industry. Universities have a wealth of resources available to them, including human and intellectual capital, and R&D infrastructure. So the front-door policies, web-portals and easy to navigate licensing policies all expedite the ability of private industry and startups to identify university R&D with commercial potential earlier and open up opportunities for companies to easily commence strategic partnerships with universities. Companies of all ages, sizes, and geographic proximity are benefiting from this invigorated support from universities. And better use of the universities physical infrastructure, such as lab space utilization with industry, reduces risks and provides valuable research opportunities to their faculty and students. By collaborating with universities and colleges, companies are able to take advantage of their well-equipped labs and breadth of skills.

Universities with specific strengths in the areas of manufacturing or energy research have established long-term partnerships with large corporations, such as BMW®, FedEx®, Johnson Controls®, IBM®, Cisco®, Proctor & Gamble®, and Minova® (Box 4.1). These relationships allow students and faculty to engage in cutting-edge research while helping solve industry problems. There is, however, some concern among a few universities that partnerships with large companies may limit a university's research options to only those areas of interest to industry. Tulane University, as an example, works to establish partnerships with smaller local companies not only to support the university's research but also to engage with the local community in a mutually beneficial way.

Box 4.1. Clemson University's International Center for Automotive Research (CU-ICAR)

CU-ICAR is an advanced-technology research campus where university, industry, and government organizations collaborate. In the university's labs and testing facilities, automotive, motorsports, aerospace, and mobility experts work together on R&D. The Center's focus on applied education and direct engagement with industry leaders includes cutting-edge curriculum development and research capabilities focused on current trends and related issues in the automotive industry. Partners, such as BMW®, Michelin®, and Koyo® work, with students and faculty to focus on systems engineering through automotive R&D.

Additionally, universities are doing a better job making their facilities, lab space and infrastructure available to private industry. This has taken many forms, from contract research and licensing agreements to Entrepreneur-In-Residence programs where investors and corporate send their brightest minds into academia for a time to understand the latest research and assess the business model and economic implications of the latest technologies.

Regardless of whether universities opt to partner with large or small businesses, collaborative efforts between universities and the private sector capitalize on the variety of resources available to both, and efforts range from individual projects to broader engagement across disciplines. Companies reap benefits from sharing laboratory and incubator space that pull together the combined intellectual capital of industry and academic experts (Box 4.2). In the later stages of technology development and commercialization, universities benefit from industry experience in areas such as market research and public relations. Furthermore, university-industry partnerships create a direct connection that facilitates job placement and talent recruitment.

Box 4.2. Examples of University-Industry Partnerships

University of Minnesota's IPrime (Industrial Partnership for Research in Interfacial and Materials Engineering) was created in 2000 and is a university/industry partnership based on two-way knowledge transfer. The partnership is a consortium of more than 40 companies supporting fundamental collaborative research on materials. Participation in IPrime affords companies the chance to scan a wide range of scientific and technological developments and delve into the fundamental science that undergirds their products. A principal goal of IPrime is the engagement of industrial scientists and engineers in a pre-competitive, non-proprietary and collaborative environment that promotes hands-on participation by visiting industrial scientists with IPrime faculty, students, and post-doctoral associates.

Northeastern University is leveraging its strong relationship with 3,600 companies through cooperative education and work programs, as well as with the privately-endowed Center for Research Innovation and Business School, to create a robust pipeline of innovation going from lab to market at startups and large companies around the world.

Universities, as regional hubs of innovation and entrepreneurship, are developing creative ways to draw industry partners to campus (Box 4.3).

Emerging trends to increase industry presence on campus and facilitate conversations on new ideas and technology include web portals that provide industry with access to university resources, networking events, such as breakfast forums and casual roundtable discussions, and structured/intensive student and faculty internships in the private sector. Industry speaker series are another popular tool for engaging university and industry scientists in discussions of commercialization opportunities available in the private sector. On some campuses, students and faculty members participate in semester-long internships with industry to learn and solve scientific and technology development challenges (Box 4.4). While these "experiential" learning opportunities for university researchers are often geared toward industry interests in areas such as medicine, natural gas drilling, green energy, pharmaceuticals, and aerospace engineering, they provide technology assistance, workforce training, and education on current market trends.

Box 4.3. University of Delaware's Office of Economic Innovation & Partnership (OEIP)

OEIP has established partnerships with the College of Engineering and the Lerner College of Business to establish a program entitled Spin InTM. The program works with local entrepreneurs who 'spin in' a technology, patent, or product that needs further development. OEIP then recruits an interdisciplinary team of undergraduate students from the business and engineering colleges to further develop the product. At the end of a pre-determined period of time, the intent is to spin the product back out to the entrepreneur for potential commercialization. OEIP also offers undergraduate and graduate student internships in the areas of technology transfer and business development.

Box 4.4. University of Minnesota's Medical Device Center's Innovation Fellows Program

This program offers a full immersion educational and product development program for medical device creation. Annual cross-functional teams are created with participants having degrees in engineering, medicine, and/or biosciences along with a demonstrated evidence of innovation and product development. Team members, or fellows, are immersed in an intense training program with access to first-class lab facilities in engineering and medical research across campus. The fellows interface daily with faculty, medical professionals, industry collaborators, and the university's technology transfer office to develop, test, patent, and license new medical devices with the goal to improve health care worldwide.

An emerging trend is the use of targeted websites and social media around current research project information and patent licensing opportunities through online databases, and the creation of network banks of past campus-wide efforts and partnerships. Some universities have implemented an external-facing portal, or an open web-based database, that provides content on innovation and commercialization processes to self-registered users and business partners. Others, such as the University of Missouri have developed tools like Source Link - online tools to highlight educational resources on campus so that businesses can easily find university experts of interest to them. These portals house all relevant information in one location, which reduces search times and increases efficiency in identifying potential commercial opportunities. By increasing openness and transparency, industry can easily access university resources and information without having to search through multiple university records.

Box 4.5. University of Michigan's Business Engagement Center (BEC)

The BEC, affiliated with the Office of the Vice President for Research and the Office of University Development, provides companies with a one-stop gateway to the various research, technology, education, facilities, and talent resources at U-M. Founded in 2007, the BEC maintains relationships with more than 1,000 companies, and is contacted by about 200 new companies each year. BEC-facilitated relationships can range from individual research projects to broader engagements, depending on the business need. One of the functions of the BEC is to work with schools and departments to encourage industry sponsorship of research at U-M. Another BEC initiative specifically aims to spur innovation and economic development in partnership with industry and government. For example, Boeing maintains a long-standing partnership with U-M, recruits from seven different U-M programs, provides support for 50 students, regularly sponsors student projects, and conducts research with four different departments.

Accelerators

Another emerging trend is the development of "accelerators" and related initiatives, located in and around university campuses (Box 4.6). These accelerators are partnerships between universities and companies that are designed to fast-track the innovation and commercialization process by providing access to world-class scientific facilities, technical personnel, and testing and diagnostics equipment— resources not readily available to many startups. Some accelerators focus on helping companies in the post-incubation period such as meeting the technical needs of startups, and bridging funding gaps.

Box 4.6. Georgia Tech's – Flashpoint

Flashpoint is a startup accelerator that offers entrepreneurial education and access to experienced mentors, experts, and investors in an immersive, shared-learning, and open workspace. The program, the first public-private partnership of its type in the country, brings together resources from the university, private sector, and startup leaders to accelerate innovation and growth. A $1 million fund, created by an investment firm working with Atlanta angel investors, invests between $15,000 and $25,000 in startup funds a company. In January 2011, Flashpoint held its first "demo day" with 15 startups from the initial Flashpoint group that included Georgia Tech faculty and students.

Providing Guidance on Intellectual Property Rights and Royalties

University partnerships often face issues in navigating intellectual property (IP) ownership of technology that is developed collaboratively with industry. However, most universities and companies are looking beyond these barriers and proactively addressing ownership issues. As more university researchers partner with industry for financial R&D support, negotiating a functional IP policy is becoming an important issue. To increase these partnerships, some universities have developed a standard policy and agreements that they use with all industry collaborators. A few universities have followed the Pennsylvania State University model, which uses a simple, flexible agreement that often leads to granting sole IP rights to the industry partner. The University of Minnesota has a unique approach in eliminating the need for protracted negotiations over IP by allowing the sponsoring company to pre-pay a fee and receive an exclusive worldwide license, and all associated royalties. By taking a flexible approach to negotiations, universities are trying to encourage more industry partnerships.

To increase transparency and encourage industry cooperation, universities are establishing unified and structured IP policies. These policies guide decisions on issues such as rights to IP and division of royalties. Some larger universities, for example, have established policies that waive a substantial portion of royalties—in some cases 25 to 35 percent—on disclosures to the sponsoring industry. Generally this has happened for industries that are quickly evolving in the global economy – where business model becomes more important than IP protection. Many universities also are creating standard forms that outline university and industry responsibilities and profit-sharing. These new IP strategies reduce uncertainty, alleviating the financial concerns that surround university-industry partnerships.

V. Engaging with Regional and Local Economic Development Efforts

Universities are proven assets to regional economies, providing employment opportunities and skilled labor, and contributing to local demand for goods and services. Likewise, universities and colleges understand that investments in surrounding communities are of benefit to their institutions. Local communities with a higher living standard can offer a diversity of good economic, housing and recreational opportunities. This attracts faculty, students, and skilled workers to the university and maintains a healthy local economy. To improve this relationship, universities are broadening their relationships with regional and local governments, businesses, and workers, while improving access to university-based resources. Today, universities are often active partners in regional economic planning and revitalization efforts.[20]

Universities have taken varied approaches to advance state, regional, and local economic development and growth objectives, including:

[20] In fact, in a 2009 AUTM survey, more than half of technology transfer offices indicated that they "frequently" or "always" had economic development responsibilities. See AUTM, "FY2009 AUTM Transaction Survey: A Survey of Non-licensing Activity of Technology Transfer Offices." See, http://www.autm.net/AM/Template.cfm? Section=Documents&Template=/CM/ContentDisplay.cfm&ContentID=5794.

Encouraging direct university participation in local businesses and communities;

Collaborating with local governments, industry, and other stakeholders to develop comprehensive approaches for regional innovation and economic development; and

Linking local communities with support networks that include federal and state governments, industry, venture capitalists, and other stakeholders.

State, regional, and local governments are also providing support to facilitate university and business interactions, such as designing regulations, laws, policies, and programs that promote responsible innovation and economic development goals.

Working Directly with Local Businesses and Communities

Universities and colleges are encouraging student and faculty education, innovation, and entrepreneurial pursuits that revitalize local businesses and address other local development needs (Box 5.1). Students and faculty are engaging directly with local businesses and communities more than ever. Universities are incorporating volunteer requirements into their curricula and encouraging students to shadow, or consult for, local businesses and non-profit organizations. Some universities are even acquiring local small businesses and allowing students to manage and operate them to hone their entrepreneurial skills. Such programs cut business costs, while providing students with hands-on learning experiences which make them more competitive in the job market.

Box 5.1. Examples of Direct Student Engagement in Local Community Businesses and Projects

Tulane University's Social Innovation and Social Entrepreneurship Initiatives integrate the entire school with the surrounding economic and social ecosystem, contributing to local economic development. Partnering with all schools including the AB Freeman School of Business, School of Architecture, and School of Science and Engineering, the program has created many student-led organizations and social ventures that assist with moving students out of the classroom and into the New Orleans Community.

Tulane has also created several university competitions including the

Tulane Business Plan Competition, the Urban Innovation Challenge, PitchNOLA, and the NewDay Social Innovation Challenge to engage students and community partners with local problems while providing them with financial and technical support to create solutions. These programs offer students the opportunity to access over $100,000 in funding annually.

Purdue University's Technical Assistance Projects bring faculty and graduate students together to provide cost-free consulting and assistance to local groups on business and technical issues.

University of Georgia's service-learning program offers enhanced courses at all of the University's schools and colleges to encourage students to provide service to the local community during their time at the university.

University of Kansas' RedTire initiative was developed to help link graduate students and alumni with struggling, local small/medium-sized businesses to prevent shuttering with ensuing loss of community services and tax base. Through this collaborative effort, businesses are able to receive support and mentorship to grow the business and employ more fellow Kansans.

The Merrimack Valley Sandbox's Campus Catalyst program provides small grants of up to $500 for students of the University of Massachusetts Lowell, Merrimack College, Middlesex Community College, and Northern Essex Community College to start entrepreneurial projects off-campus and in their communities.

Faculty members also support local communities through teaching, mentoring, and initiatives to advance innovation and economic development goals. Many university programs are working to foster dialogue between faculty and the local community to tackle local challenges. As faculty engage in R&D, they increasingly collaborate with regional stakeholders to push technology development forward and open the door to viable market opportunities locally. These efforts have led to long-term partnerships with local communities.

Collaborative Approaches for Achieving Regional Economic Development

Universities are engaging in long-term, dedicated innovation and entrepreneurship efforts that promote regional and local economic development. They are working closely with community stakeholders—government, companies, venture capitalists, entrepreneurs, and workers—to improve access to university-based assets and to implement regional innovation and economic strategies. Universities use a variety of collaborative models, including research parks, university corridors, startup accelerators, shared laboratory space, incubators, and innovation and manufacturing clusters. These venues bring together infrastructure and intellectual capital to address innovation and business challenges and to develop local economies. These efforts provide a cost-effective and productive means for conducting research, developing technology, and spurring new markets and businesses.

Universities are well positioned to contribute greatly to these efforts. The universities capitalize on the power of proximity, building research parks locally, which help to revitalize downtown areas or once-thriving communities. Research parks house technology transfer and strategic partnership offices, and incubator and accelerator spaces. They also host entrepreneurs-in-residence, provide mentoring opportunities, connect individuals with similar research interests, and assist with the licensing and commercialization processes.

Startup incubators and accelerators hosted by universities serve as powerful places for local community members to start new companies and solve pressing local and national innovation and commercialization challenges. Incubators focus on addressing local community issues such as supporting local startups by providing mentorship and technical support, thus contributing to local economies.

Box 5.2. Examples of Regional Corridors

University of California, Lawrence Berkeley's East Bay Green Corridor is a broad regional collaboration to support the emerging clean technology economy. It builds upon the region's existing strength as a center for emerging green technology, innovation, and entrepreneurship.

Pennsylvania State University I-99 Corridor Region has received funding from the NSF Partnership for Innovation program and the Commonwealth to leverage Penn State research and education strengths for job creation in nearby counties of Bedford, Blair, and Centre.

University of Michigan's University Research Corridor (URC) is an alliance between Michigan State University, the University of Michigan and Wayne State University to transform, strengthen and diversify the state's economy.

Iowa State University's Research Corridor stretches from Ames to De Moines and focuses on research and manufacturing in agriculture, metals, and other areas. ISU and technology companies such as DuPont® and Syngenta® contribute their expertise toward the effort.

Universities also are encouraging economic development through the creation of research corridors. These corridors reside within and across regions and often have a particular technology focus, such as biotechnology, nanotechnology, health, energy and advanced materials. Corridors offer a resource pipeline for local communities, universities, and colleges that have similar research interests and challenges. They attract industry by providing technical support, access to capital, and a large network of experts. Some research corridors unite communities across state lines, which allow them to address issues of regional importance, such as green technology, job training for the unemployed, and small business creation. Furthermore, corridors also produce regional economic analyses with information on regional economies, such as numbers on job growth, state income, and state startups. Job creation is also an important focus of many research corridors. Overall, universities are extending their influence and better serving their communities by participating in research corridors that connect them with other local universities, thereby leveraging the talent and resources of all of the participating institutions.

Finally, universities are an excellent source of economic, regional, and business development data and analysis, ranging from tracking regional economic development and growth to providing data on university, federal and other resources available to local communities. Many universities are working together with faculty, staff, students, and community leaders to find, highlight, and solve regional issues. The U.S. Economic Development Administration's University Center's Program has supported centers in all fifty states to create this sort of data.

Regional Technology Transfer Centers

As mentioned in Section IV, several regions have created regional technology transfer centers in order to coordinate commercialization of R&D conducted at their universities, and in collaboration with other universities and labs. These regional centers were created for two reasons – for universities to assist each other in the commercialization of innovation that was done across institutions, and to keep innovative ideas in their respective regions. For example, the Massachusetts Technology Transfer Center is an initiative that provides technology transfer services to multiple colleges and universities in the area that are not research-driven. In addition, it has played an important role in keeping innovators and entrepreneurs in the region – particularly those not affiliated with a large research university. Many regional economic development plans call for this type of collaboration to retain regional talent and innovation.

Linking Local Communities to Support Networks

Universities engaging more in developing and implementing regional economic strategies are undertaking a predominant role in linking local businesses and community leaders with national and regional support networks to expand the pool of available resources. Universities hold a unique position in local communities. They can provide a venue where all stakeholders, including researchers, venture capitalists, companies, entrepreneurs, consultants and regional authorities and organizations, can come together to tackle critical local issues, such as locating grant and other funding opportunities (Box 5.3). Universities are also a good source of intellectual capital.

Box 5.3. Missouri KC - Whiteboard to Boardroom

This bi-state (Missouri and Kansas) partnership of regional colleges, universities, community colleges, local businesses, and nonprofits seeks to discover and develop technology by pulling it out of the institutions and actively moving it along the development pathway. Through this program, students, faculty, and local community work to establish new business ventures, licensing opportunities, create jobs, and spur economic development through mentoring, job training, hands on learning opportunities, and access to capital funds. Through the collaborative effort, partnerships are expanded to form and encourage technology growth and business plan development for the local economy.

A number of university economic development efforts have targeted underserved communities, such as programs supporting women and minority entrepreneurs to help increase economic development opportunities across the region (Box 5.4).

Box 5.4. Examples of Reaching Underserved Communities

University of California, Berkeley has students from its Center for Young Entrepreneurs at Haas (YEAH) work in the community with underprivileged East Bay and Bay Area youth to share best practices in entrepreneurship, a passion for education, and to help high school students in the area pursue a college education.

Texas State's RampCorp program works to improve economic opportunities for women entrepreneurs in Texas. Women entrepreneurs receive coaching from experienced investors, entrepreneurs, inventors, and business leaders to learn about resources and opportunities. The RampCorp program includes both skills and knowledge training to provide guidance in starting, growing, and funding scalable companies.

Other Efforts to Provide Incentives to Promote an Innovation Economy

State and local governments help to provide resources and design laws, regulations, and initiatives that can promote innovation and regional economic development. Recent trends show that state and local governments are pairing up with universities to stimulate local economies through research and business investments, workforce development, and job creation. By joining forces, both parties maximize the use of their resources. For example, to stimulate local innovation, state and local government offer regional grants that match funding that universities contribute. With these additional resources, advancements in green technology, health sciences, manufacturing, and infrastructure can be applied to solve local challenges while creating jobs.

These collaborative efforts help align resources and support with state and local needs and strengths.

Many states have begun to incentivize regional innovation and economic development by expanding private sector investments in local communities through tax cuts and other benefits. State-sponsored angel networks and venture funds are taking a larger role in the commercialization of technology and the creation of startups. Some states fund their venture capital programs by auctioning tax credits.

Targeted state-level innovation tax credits for local projects also encourage local investment to keep development of early-stage technology and companies within the region.

Many universities are also hoping that the recent guidance by the U.S. Department of Treasury about program related investing will entice a greater number of foundations and charitable trusts to invest directly in entrepreneurs and in university programs that nurture startup creation. Charitable foundations often focus on regions or specific topical areas, and their ability to fund innovation and entrepreneurship to meet the needs could be a critical new source of funding for these efforts.

Conclusion: Recognizing the Growing Number of Economically-engaged Universities

In addition to the five areas highlighted above, the NACIE-sponsored university presidents' letter had a sixth focus category – the recognition of exemplary economic engagement by universities. The letter suggested that more should be done to recognize those universities that are truly breaking new ground by supporting innovation and entrepreneurship in the realm of economic development. We hope that this report is the first step in an on-going recognition and celebration of university-based innovation and entrepreneurship.

While the letter itself had a profound impact on the higher education community, it also highlighted the need to understand the details of university-based innovation and entrepreneurship to assist in the development of future ideas and programs in this space. The goal of the letter was to lay out, programmatically, how major research universities were nurturing innovation and entrepreneurship – organized in the five focus categories of the letter. In addition, the letter identified some of the more common practices, such as business plan contests, as well as collaborative activities that universities should engage in, such as a database, mapping research and patent applications. This was important because most major research universities and colleges in the U.S. are not yet performing these activities. The letter has become a road map for aspiring universities and colleges around the country that are looking for a path forward for nurturing innovation and entrepreneurship.

The examples cited in this report, and the underlying discussion, underscored the diversity of approaches by higher education institutions across the United States for promoting innovation and entrepreneurship. This diversity reflects not only the history, research funding, location, and size of a particular institution, but also helps the reader understand what the role of outside actors, such as government, investors, and entrepreneurs should be in order to create more university- and college- sponsored spinoffs. The hope is that this report will serve as a source of ideas and encourage connections between peers with similar objectives and circumstances. In other words, as universities strategize about the next generation of innovation programs that they would like to launch, this report should help them identify peer institutions that have already implemented similar programs.

Finally, the university community is keen on expanding and improving its partnerships with the federal government. For every best practice or emerging trend in innovative programs that this report highlighted, there are a similar number of recommendations to improve public policy and federal funding programs to help universities commercialize more of their R&D and ideas. Furthermore, as the Presidential Memorandum on Technology Transfer is implemented, a discussion on synergies and challenges to align the goals, missions, and opportunities between federal agencies and universities is certain to arise. The results of those discussions will have a tremendously positive impact on the U.S. economy and prospects for job creation.

As innovation and entrepreneurship becomes an even greater force in economic growth, U.S. universities and colleges will be the vanguard in discovering that innovation and in nurturing the entrepreneurs that can create products, services, economic value, and high-quality jobs. While this report identifies a series of practices that are helping universities become better at this, there are many more examples that could have been highlighted. OIE looks forward to working with the higher education community to identify and promote those practices in future reports.

APPENDIX: "DEEP DIVES" OF SELECTED COLLEGES AND UNIVERSITIES

In April 2010, over 140 leaders from higher education endorsed and submitted a letter to then Commerce Secretary Locke through his National Advisory Council on Innovation and Entrepreneurship (NACIE). They committed to work more closely with industry, private foundations, investors, and local, state, and federal governments to enhance efforts to promote innovation, entrepreneurship, and the commercialization of research results. Underlining their commitment was a willingness to employ strategies, enhance existing activities, and expand efforts in several areas, including:

- Promoting Student Innovation and Entrepreneurship,
- Encouraging Faculty Innovation and Entrepreneurship,
- Actively Supporting the University Technology Transfer Function,
- Facilitating University – Industry Collaboration, and
- Engaging with Regional and Local Economic Development Efforts.

The Office of Innovation and Entrepreneurship (OIE) recently followed up with each signatory to better understand their efforts to embody and implement the ideas contained within the letter, as well as to improve our ability to develop policies and programs that support innovation, entrepreneurship, and the commercialization of research results. OIE is conducting phones calls with every respondent to discuss their strategies and develop a general outline of each of their initiatives.

For a select few institutions, including some who have not signed the NACIE letter, OIE has conducted a more thorough exploration of their strategies and initiatives. The goals of these "deep dives" is to discuss the historical and cultural context for the relevant work being done at leading institutions, highlight innovative practices, and uncover future trends. These institutions include:

1. Arkansas Baptist College
2. Alabama State University
3. Arizona State University
4. Georgia Institute of Technology
5. Howard University
6. Lorain County Community College

7. University of Michigan – Ann Arbor
8. University of North Carolina – Chapel Hill
9. Prairie View A&M University
10. William Marsh Rice University
11. University of Southern California

Entrepreneurship, Innovation, & Commercialization of Research at Arkansas Baptist College

Overview – Rebuilding Lives & Local Community[21]

Arkansas Baptist College (ABC) is a private, historically black liberal arts college located in Little Rock, Arkansas. ABC was founded in 1884 as the Minister's Institute, and was initially funded by the Colored Baptists of the State of Arkansas.

ABC's current president, Dr. Fitzgerald "Fitz" Hill, is the 13th president in the school's history. Dr. Hill accepted his presidency at a time when no salary was budgeted to pay him, and school enrollment had dipped to fewer than 200 students. Under Dr. Hill's leadership, enrollment has since grown to more than 1,100 students. The school's budget has grown from $2 million to nearly $20 million, and Dr. Hill now draws a salary[i].

Dr. Hill is committed to nurturing ABC's traditional strengths as a historically black college: connecting academic programs to applied workforce and entrepreneurial skills and taking a leading role in rebuilding the local community.

The Community Union, an 11,000-square-foot facility scheduled to open later in 2012, a renovated Old Main residence hall, and two new education buildings, are part of an over $30 million capital campaign now underway at Arkansas Baptist College.

Arkansas Baptist College's (ABC) *Scott Ford Center for Entrepreneurship and Community Development*[ii] is ABC's flagship entrepreneurship initiative. In addition to a micro-lending program, the Center will offer *the Icehouse Project*, a special course designed to immerse participants in eight life-lessons in fundamental concepts to building an entrepreneurial mindset. ABC is one of the initial pilot sites for the Icehouse Project, which was developed by Pulitzer Prize-nominee Clifton Taulbert and

[21] Comments By Howard O. Gibson, Ph.D. Interim Vice President for Academic Affairs; Dean, School of Business; Director, Center for Entrepreneurship - Arkansas Baptist

Gary Schoeniger. *The Ewing Marion Kauffman Foundation and the Foundation of Entrepreneurship*, which focuses on entrepreneurship, innovation, and education provides funding for Icehouse Project.

The *African Bean Company* is another key partner in the Scott Ford Center. African Bean Company manufactures the Roots Java coffee brand, which sells coffee beans harvested in Africa. Currently, the African Bean Company is negotiating retail agreements with major retailers throughout the country. Profits from sales will assist ABC in its capital campaign. The college will house a Roots Java retail outlet in the Community Union building.

Below is an enumeration of Arkansas Baptist College programs and initiatives that support the five buckets in the NACIE sponsored university commitment letter.

Student Entrepreneurship

Entrepreneurship is one of three concentrations in the School of Business's Department of Business Administration; it offers students an opportunity to start a new business, run a family business, or launch a new venture within an existing company. The program provides students with the knowledge, skills, and abilities needed to enter the entrepreneurial field. The concentration is also designed to provide students with the drive, motivation, and discipline required to handle challenges associated with starting or building a business.

In addition to academic work, business students can join the Entrepreneurship Club and deepen their practical knowledge by co-managing various college owned businesses. The Entrepreneurship Club aims to provide a conduit for students to access relevant entrepreneurial resources, network with prominent community entrepreneurs, and share ideas. To this end, the Club is dedicated to building further understanding about new or small businesses, and about entrepreneurship in all businesses. To deepen their practical knowledge, students have opportunities to participate in internships and service learning projects at the ABC's Garden of Eden. This type of learning allows students to apply knowledge and skills in a real-world setting. Through these experiences, students deepen knowledge, build workplace skills, and come to better understand the world in all its complexities.

Faculty Entrepreneurship

ABC business school faculty will participate in the Scott Ford Center for Entrepreneurship and Community Development's initiatives to train entrepreneurs to start businesses in underserved communities. The faculty will work with student organizations to build and cultivate relationships and to increase campus awareness of entrepreneurial thinking and opportunities. The faculty will also collaborate with the Director of Career Planning and Placement to provide an entrepreneurial perspective to Careers Services initiatives. In using the Center as a service portal, the faculty will network with already successful businesses and business support agencies in the area and surrounding area. The purpose of the Center involves establishing a network of mentors and resources for start-up and existing businesses or community residents who are interested business ownership.

Dr. Howard O. Gibson, Dean of the School of Business and Director of Entrepreneurship leads the ABC's faculty entrepreneurship initiative. Dr. Gibson and the faculty will co-manage the Center's microenterprise loan fund, which will serve as a catalyst to spur business development in core urban areas.

University Technology Transfer Functions

ABC does not have a technology transfer office in the conventional sense. However, the College hopes the entrepreneurial capital graduates will positively transform the local business climate. In this way, rather than commercializing research outputs, the College hopes to add to the entrepreneurial vigor of its community through college and alumni owned business ventures.

College-Industry Collaboration

ABC's Capital Campaign and various entrepreneurship initiatives have deepened the College's collaborations with the private industry. These collaborative relationships include *First Security Bank of Little Rock* and *Arkansas Capital Corporation.*

First Security Bank of Little Rock and Arkansas Capital Corporation will provide financing for ABC's $18 million capital improvement initiative[iii]. Under the New Markets Tax Credit Program, the Arkansas Capital Corporation will sell tax credits to qualified national investors, and the tax credits ultimately will reduce the amount of debt owed by ABC to First Security Bank.

Over the past two years, ABC has raised $6 million in contributions and grants for capital projects. The College has also demolished or renovated 20 houses, bought 12 additional homes and lots, and acquired three businesses in an effort to revitalize the neighborhood.

As part of the capital improvement, ABC has:

- Constructed a new building that will expand the cafeteria from 77 seats to 322
- Constructed a new 190-bed residence hall; and
- Purchased land around the campus to prepare for future growth. ABC will also:
- Construct a community union that will include a coffee shop, a campus bookstore, a lounge-study area, a food court, a conference room, and office spaces.

Another invaluable industry collaboration is with *Ewing Marion Kauffman Foundation and the Foundation of Entrepreneurship*. These two organizations will co-fund ABC's Icehouse Project.

Regional and Local Economic Development

The *Scott Ford Center for Entrepreneurship and Community Development* will be recognized as an innovator in educating and serving students and clients in economic development. In addition, the Center will become a catalyst for development in Little Rock and beyond. The design of the Center is a blended model using a micro-enterprise development process through business education. This process will combine the best practices in this generation of revenue and social-value to educate and train social entrepreneurs for the twenty-first century.

ABC through *the Scott Ford Center for Entrepreneurship and Community Development*[iv], will house a micro-lending program to provide small business loans to individuals who might not otherwise qualify. The micro-enterprise loan fund will serve as a catalyst to spur business development in core urban areas. An independent board that includes the College's business faculty and administration, and local experts in banking and venture capital will supervise the pilot fund.

- Lending will range from $50 loans to up to $5,000;
- The program aims to launch up to 10 new businesses annually; and
- Borrowers will be able to draw on the expertise of the advisory council in developing their business strategy.

In addition, ABC also operates several community businesses. These include the *Auto Baptism Car Wash* and the *Garden of Eden Fresh Market*. All the businesses supported by ABC serve as a training ground for its students. In turn, the College reinvests the profits to restore the surrounding neighborhood.

Conclusion

The revitalization of Arkansas Baptist College (ABC) has been both innovative and entrepreneurial. In February 2006, ABC's enrollment was fewer than 200 students, and the college appeared on the verge of losing its accreditation. Five years later, ABC has a new men's residence facility, which houses nearly 200 students, along with a soon to be completed women's residence hall.

Improvements have not been limited to physical structures; ABC has maintained its accreditation by the North Central Higher Learning Commission and enrollment has grown to more than 1,100 students. The school's budget has also grown from $2 million to nearly $20 million.

ABC's success was crafted by Dr. Hill's innovative vision of creating a non-traditional entrepreneurial school which welcomes everyone. The college assists high school dropouts (up to 40 percent of urban students currently drop out) to earn a GED. Successful candidates can then enroll full-time at ABC. Dr. Hill has also set on an aggressive $36 million capital campaign, which has already raised $23 million. Even so, tuition is about $2,700 a semester, making ABC the least expensive private school in Arkansas[v].

Just as importantly, many of the initiatives that account for ABC's success can be replicated in many HBCU and urban universities.

Dr. Gibson's comments have been instructive in better understanding ABC's various innovative entrepreneurship programs. As well as the impact of the NACIE commitment letter in framing ABC's strategic plans and institutional culture.

The Office of Innovation and Entrepreneurship thanks ABC's assistance with this case study, and looks forward to a continued close and collaborative relationship in building America's innovation infrastructure.

Entrepreneurship, Innovation, & Commercialization of Research at the Alabama State University (ASU)

Overview — Motivate & Inspire, Especially the Underserved[22]

Alabama State University, founded 1867, is a historically black university located in Montgomery, Alabama. Under the leadership of President William H. Harris, the university continues its role as a purveyor of innovative scholarship, especially in the African American community. Alabama State University considers the NACIE commitment letter as an affirmation of the school's historical role, and current initiatives to make entrepreneurship a core part of its future strategy.

Breaking with orthodoxy, Alabama State University requires faculty to enhance their theoretical knowledge of entrepreneurship with practical experience, through summer internship with entrepreneurs. Entrepreneurship has also moved from the exclusive domain of the College of Business Administration (COBA) to become part of a larger university culture. The COBA students are now also allowed the option of choosing either an international business, or entrepreneurship concentration. More recently, the College of Visual & Performing Arts, Health Sciences, and the Communications Department have added entrepreneurship curriculum.

The Center for Entrepreneurship, Innovation, and Change's (CEIC) Entrepreneur-In- Residence Lecture Series introduces and motivates student participation in, and understanding of, entrepreneurship. CEIC also sponsors the attendance of 80 College of Business Administration students at the Allen Entrepreneurial Institute in Lithonia, GA. This institute teaches professional etiquette, public speaking, and other educational activities to augment student preparation for business ownership or corporate employment.

The College of Business Administration's partnership with CEIC extends beyond the university gates. Through their jointly administered International Business Summer Camp, 14 rising junior and senior high school students, from rural Alabama, were brought to ASU campus for training. The students were also taken on an international excursion to the Bahamas to further challenge their imagination and international exposure. A second High School

---

[22] Comments by: Ms. Janel Bell Haynes, Chair, Business Administration Department, Alabama State University; Dr. Le-Quita J Booth, Dean, College of Business Administration/Director, the Disadvantaged Businesses Enterprise (DBE), Alabama State University; Dr. Kamal Hingorani, Chair of Computer Information Systems, Alabama State University; and Dr. William Pickard, Entrepreneur in Residence, Alabama State University, Chairman and CEO of Global Automotive Alliance, LLC.

Summer Boot Camp brought rising juniors and seniors from an urban setting (Detroit, MI), to entrepreneurship and college readiness immersion camp.

Another initiative at COBA's Center for Disadvantaged Business Enterprises/Supportive Services provides On-The-Job Training programs and other services to minority owned Highway Construction businesses. Through On-The-Job Training, the Center retrains displaced minority workers in Highway Construction. Additionally, COBA's Small Business Development Center (SBDC) provides broader technical and management assistance to small businesses and prospective business owners.

In the spirit of the NACIE commitment letter, ASU's membership in the Alabama Automotive Manufacturers Association (AAMA) facilitates a collaborative relationship with local industry. The university organizes faculty and student study-tours, seminars, and workshops with local manufacturers. These include Hyundai, Mercedes Benz, Honda assembly plants, and ThyssenKrupp.

Student Entrepreneurship

Through a curriculum that combines theoretical and practical interdisciplinary learning, ASU offers an Entrepreneurship Minor for both Business and non-Business Major students. Additionally, *the Center of Excellence for Entrepreneurship* in the *College of Business Administration (COBA)*, in close cooperation with accomplished and successful entrepreneurs, inspires and teaches the entrepreneurial spirit to students through several programs that will contribute to the economic development of the state of Alabama and the broader southern region. These programs include:

- The Entrepreneur-in-Residence Lecture Series, pairs some of the most successful entrepreneurs in the black community with ASU's student entrepreneurs in vibrant practitioner lecture series;
- Women in Business Experience, provides coaching, training and peer support for women-owned businesses through various stages of development; and
- Development of Communities, targets communities within 2 miles of the ASU campus to address blighted conditions, and infuse ASU's entrepreneurial spirit to improve various sectors including residential and commercial housing.

The Center of Excellence for International Business[vi] will internationalize ASU's innovation and entrepreneurship by providing opportunities for faculty, students, and the business community to develop and broaden their international business expertise and cross-cultural understanding.

- Foreign Study Tours: Implement overseas week-long study-tours to South Korea and China with assistance from ASU's global university partners–the ChungAng University in Seoul, Korea; and the Fudan University in Shanghai, China;
- Domestic Study Tours: Organize study-tours for students and faculty to seminars, workshops, and manufacturing facilities (such as Hyundai, Mercedes Benz, Honda, and ThyssenKrupp) within the state of Alabama that involve global business; and
- NASBITE Certified Global Business Professional Club (CGBP): Establish a student club that will foster an educational and cultural environment in which students who have an interest in international business and CGBP certification can share ideas and experiences.

In addition to these initiatives, *the College of Business Administration (COBA) & the Center for Entrepreneurship, Innovation, and Change* (CEIC) will host *the Business Empowerment Series* on Thursday, March 15, 2012 from 5pm – 7pm.

Faculty Entrepreneurship

ASU faculty members will also benefit from the *Center of Excellence for International Business* through the following entrepreneurship initiatives:

- FDIB: Provide faculty training in international business (through CIBERs and other programs) to facilitate higher standards in teaching and research;
- Promote faculty development and research in International Business;
- Seminar Series: Organize quarterly seminars conducted by experts on International Business both from academia and industry; and
- Trade Missions: Support faculty participation in Governor of Alabama's trade and business development missions.

University Technology Transfer Functions

ASU does not have a tech transfer office in the conventional sense. However, *The Small Business Development Center* (SBDC)[vii] at ASU provides technical and management assistance to small businesses and prospective business owners. As an institutional member of the Alabama Small Business

Development NETWORK the SBDC is one of twelve University-based business assistance sources located throughout the state of Alabama.

The SBDC is committed to providing quality technology transfer services, in addition to other functions to businesses in an eight-county catchment area including—Autauga, Bullock, Chambers, Coosa, Elmore, Lowndes, Montgomery, and Tallapoosa counties—in Central Alabama.

In addition, *the Center of Excellence for International Business* has been instrumental in ASU becoming one of the few universities that have won the prestigious *Business and International Education* grant from the *US Department of Education* for two consecutive cycles.

University-Industry Collaboration

The Center of Excellence for International Business also plays a crucial role in ASU-industry collaboration. The Center will conduct the following:

- *Workshops on Exporting and Strategic Sourcing* will be conducted in association with our industry partners. These summer workshops will seek to assist SMEs with their export and strategic sourcing
- *Roundtables on Global Accounting Issues* will include roundtables that focus on fundamentals and fine points of International Financial Reporting Standards (IFRS), international accounting, transfer pricing, auditing, tax issues, and how to do business in diverse regions of the world
- *New Website:* The Center will develop, host, and maintain a new web site for International Business Resources for the community

Regional and Local Economic Development

The Disadvantaged Businesses Enterprise (DBE) department within ASU's College of Business Administration is leading a major effort to increase job creation in the state of Alabama[viii]. This initiative includes a summit held January 20, 2012 to introduce the *Alabama Works, Alabama Wins* project which aims to boost competitiveness among Alabama's contractors, and therefore their ability to create jobs in the state.

As part of ASU's commitment to *Alabama Works, Alabama Wins* program, the university will establish the Emerging Contractors program. This program will among other services, provide classes for subcontractors to help them develop increased business skills for the construction industry. Subcontractors who complete the program will be placed on the bidders list for construction jobs in the state.

The *Emerging Contractors* program will adopt the curriculum that is used by the Alabama chapter of Associated Builders and Contractors Inc. (ABC).

Deep-Dive Questions

- Is innovation an integral part of ASU's institutional culture?
- Why is it important? And how does it influence entrepreneurship and tech transfer?
- How do you envision your program in the future?
- What is your vision for each of the case study's bucket?
- How does your institution leverage (or intend to leverage) geographic endowment?
- Are your innovation, entrepreneurship, and tech transfer programs integrated? — Why, or why not?
- Are there any unique successes (and or challenges) you may wish to highlight?

Conclusion

Alabama State University (ASU) is small university by population, and does not appear to have the benefit of large budgets that is common in typical Association of American Universities (AAU) member schools. It can however be argued that dollar-for-dollar, ASU derives similar levels of academic and entrepreneurial outputs with its larger counterparts.

Even so, there are lessons from larger university innovation programs in scale, impact, program rigor, and access to capital that may be applicable to ASU. The Office of Innovation & Entrepreneurship university innovation case studies should be a good starting point for ASU's faculty to compare innovative practices.

Comments by Ms. Janel Bell Haynes and her colleagues have been instructive in better understanding Alabama State University's various innovative entrepreneurship programs, as well as the impact of the NACIE commitment letter on the school's strategic plan and institutional culture.

The Office of Innovation and Entrepreneurship thanks Alabama State University's assistance with this case study, and looks forward to a continued close and collaborative relationship in building America's innovation infrastructure.

Entrepreneurship, Innovation, & Commercialization of Research at Arizona State University (ASU)

Overview – A New American University[23]

President Michael M. Crow has positioned ASU as the model for a New American University. A model that measures success not by who it excludes, but by who it includes; a model that pursues research and discovery that benefit the public good and assumes major responsibility for the economic, social and cultural vitality as well as the health and well-being of the community.

The Office of University Initiatives (UI) is a cultural catalyst at ASU. UI helps ASU meet its innovation needs by connecting ideas with people and resources to make an impact. Through collaboration with other offices and departments across the university, in addition to state, national and international leaders, UI helps to shape and realize ASU's innovation goals. Much of UI's work falls into five overlapping categories: advancing ASU's New American University agenda, entrepreneurship, social embeddedness, university innovation, and education9. UI is the chief advocate for entrepreneurial thinking and activity across the university.

The Edson Student Entrepreneurship Initiative is ASU's premier student start-up competition. This year, students can win up to $20,000 in funding, as well as mentoring and office space to advance their venture ideas. Non-profit and for-profit initiatives are both encouraged. And students have responded with a number of innovative ventures. The G3Box project focuses on converting steel shipping containers into medical grade clinics by outfitting them with the basic components of power, ventilation, potable water, and insulation to create sustainable medical clinics that address critical health needs in poor countries.

ASU has a unique two-distinct Engineering School model. *The Ira A. Fulton Schools of Engineering* is the flagship traditional school, while the *College of Technology and Innovation* embodies the values of engaged learning, including a strong connection with industry and entrepreneurship. The hands-on approach model of the latter school requires students to build and design solutions to meet real industry needs; the model appears to be making an economic impact.

The engineering firm Honeywell, recently hired all College of Technology and Innovation students who worked on a successful airplane breaking system.

---

[23] Comments by: James O'Brien, Vice President, & Chief of Staff Office Of The President

Separately from that, the city of Chandler, Arizona approved a 50-year lease with the College of Technology and Innovation. The city will retrofit a building to house the College's teaching and research programs. These programs are estimated to provide a $23.8 million economic impact in the next five years, by providing the intellectual capital for the city's high tech companies such as Intel.

Even with successful and innovative programs, about 20 percent of the university's population may not fully accept change. However, experience provides a helpful ameliorative blueprint. Consistency and a clear articulation of the president's vision usually earn the respect of skeptics. ASU's quest as a New American University has also been helped by the President's intuitive understanding of internal constituencies, and an ability to maintain enough dynamism to make concessions where necessary. President Crow has also built a capable and competent senior leadership team. Most importantly, ASU's leadership team recognizes that innovation, by necessity, means not being constrained by conventional thinking. Thus with creativity, there are no obstacles that cannot be managed.

Just as a bell, innovation without movement does not ring. So go ahead, let innovation ring - join the movement for a New American University.

Below is an enumeration of ASU's programs and initiatives that support the five buckets in the NACIE sponsored university commitment letter.

Student Entrepreneurship

At ASU, entrepreneurship is about bringing innovative ideas out into the world. These ideas might be socially, economically, artistically or intellectually motivated, or some combination thereof.

At ASU, entrepreneurship is not concentrated in just the field of business, nor is it housed in an entrepreneurial institute or school. Instead, entrepreneurship opportunities are offered in and out of the classroom, and in a wide variety of programs departments and schools. These include:

The *Edson Student Entrepreneurship Initiative*[X] that harnesses the entrepreneurial energy, excitement and creativity of ASU's student body. It provides funding, office space and training for teams of students across the university to explore their innovative ideas for business products and services. These teams typically work in partnership with faculty, researchers and successful entrepreneurs from both the academic and private sectors. The Edson Student Entrepreneur Initiative has been made possible by an investment of $5.4 million from Orin Edson to the Arizona State University Foundation.

- **Funding:** The endowment provides a total of $200,000 annually in seed funding.
    - Each year, 10 to 15 teams will be granted $5,000 to $20,000 to subsidize expenses for developing their new venture. Money granted could be used for such things as market research, building a prototype, and legal fees
- **Office Space:** Winning teams are awarded office space at *SkySong*, located in South Scottsdale, through their award year.
    - The *SkySong* facility provides a professional setting for early stage entrepreneurs to develop their ventures and also to interact and learn from peer entrepreneurs, local, and international businesses
- **Training and Coaching:** Throughout the award year teams participate in a series of workshops with guest speakers that include successful entrepreneurs and professionals with relevant expertise
    - Team members are offered entrepreneurial training courses at *SkySong* and/ or nonprofit training courses by ASU's *Center for Nonprofit Leadership and Management*. Teams are also provided ongoing entrepreneurial coaching by Edson staff.

ASU Innovation Challenge[xi] seeks undergraduate and graduate students who are dedicated to making a difference in the local and global communities through innovation. Students can win up to *$10,000* to make their innovative project, prototype, venture or community partnership ideas happen.

- Students are provided opportunities to practice their skills in teamwork, leadership, project development, business plan creation, public speaking, and network creation

The Performing Arts Venture Experience (P.A.V.E)[xii] paves the way to the future of the arts by investing in student innovation and creativity, supporting arts entrepreneurship education and undertaking entrepreneurial activities. Funded by a generous grant by the *Kauffman Foundation*, there are four major components of P.A.V.E:

- Arts entrepreneurship classes such as Foundations of Arts Entrepreneurship, Arts Entrepreneurship Seminar, Theatre Organization and Management and Independent Film;

- Investment in, and support for, student initiated arts-based ventures, both for- and not-for-profit;
- Faculty development and research in arts entrepreneurship; and
- Public programming on arts entrepreneurship including speakers, workshops and symposia.

10,000 Solutions[xiii] is a place to showcase and collect innovative ideas that solve local and global challenges. ASU views this project as an experiment that leverages the power of collaborative wisdom to create a solutions bank. The 10,000 Solutions Project explores what can be accomplished when passionate people join a community that works together to build upon each other's innovative ideas and create change.

Funding: The program is funded by *Kauffman Campuses Initiative* which supports innovation and entrepreneurship at ASU and beyond. The program provides up to $10,000 to fund good ideas from students, staff, faculty and community members.

The Cronkite School students (and faculty) are encouraged to submit ideas for *Knight News Challenge* (and won) and for *J-Lab Women Entrepreneurs* grants. Those winners are heralded as much as winners of journalism contests

ASU also strives to deliver research breakthroughs and achieve discovery in a broad range of strategic research areas including[xiv]:

- The *New Media Innovation Lab*, Operated by *the Cronkite School*, is a research and development program designed to help media companies create new and exciting multimedia products. The lab brings together students from across campus – journalism, business, computer engineering and design, to develop a variety of products, including an iPhone app and widgets and Facebook applications.
- *The ASU College of Nursing and Health Innovation* has had more than $27.5 million in awards from the National Institutes of Health (NIH) and other corporate agencies since 2005. The research focus of ASU nursing and health program provides short and longterm economic benefits. In the short term, Arizona benefits economically from grant funding. In the longer term, Arizonans benefit from medical improvements in research findings, and the commercial impact of potential tech transfer.
- *The Arizona Center for Algae Technology and Innovation* (AzCATI), located at ASU, has been a pioneer in algae research as a source of

low-cost, sustainable biofuel. The Laboratory was contracted by the Department of Energy to research and develop algae conversion.

Faculty Entrepreneurship

ASU's *The Pathways to Entrepreneurship Grant* (PEG)[xv] program provides funding to faculty/staff who wish to implement or enhance entrepreneurship curricular or co-curricular programs. The following programs all have some roots grounded in the in the Pathways to Entrepreneurship Grant.

Innovation Advancement Program at the ***Sandra Day O'Connor College of Law:*** This program provides legal and consulting services to start-up enterprises and entrepreneurs.

- Team Leader: Eric Menkus, Innovation Advancement Program Director. Amount Awarded: $90,000. Number of Grants Awarded: 2.

InnovationSpace at the ***Herberger Institute for Design and the Arts*****:** Team Leader: Prasad Boradkar, Innovation Space Program Director. Amount Awarded: $115,000. Number of Grants Awarded: 4

- Grant funding introduces students to design concepts based on resilience theory (the ability of individuals to recover from destabilizing life events, such as a serious illness) and biomimicry (design inspired by nature). Students also worked with a local company to design toys for autistic children.

The following programs are run from the ***College of Liberal Arts and Sciences:***

- ***First Innovations:*** Team Leader: Pat Mariella, American Indian Policy Institute Director. Amount Awarded: $68,000. Number of Grants Awarded: 1
  - Grantfunding provided for at wo-day workshop, which was subsequently developed into three ASU courses and a summer program for high school students.
- ***Phoenix Innovation Study*****:** Team Leader: Sander van der Leeuw, School of Human Evolution and Social Change Director. Amount Awarded: $33,000. Number of Grants Awarded: 1
  - Funded research on ethnographic study of SkySong, the ASU Scottsdale Innovation Center.

- ***Social Innovation and Social Enterprise*:** Team Leader: Vanna Gonzales, School of Social Transformation Assistant Professor. Amount Awarded: $30,000. Number of Grants Awarded: 1
  - Grant funding enables students to work with local social entrepreneurs to advance their organization's goals through innovation.

The following programs are run out of the ***College of Technology and Innovation*:**

- Global Resolve: Team Leader: Mark Henderson, Global Resolve Director. Amount Awarded: $59,000. Number of Grants Awarded: 2
  - Funds development of cap stone courses that engage students in creating ventures in developing countries using technologies that solve local challenges. These courses are now part of the core courses for the social entrepreneurship focus in the *technological entrepreneurship and management degree program.*
- Startup Weekend ASU: Team Leader: Kevin Gary, College of Technology and Innovation Associate Professor. Amount Awarded: $39,000. Number of Grants Awarded: 1
  - Funding supports the development of courses in software entrepreneurship and launched the inaugural Startup Weekend at ASU.

The *Mary Lou Fulton Teachers College* runs the *Advancing P-20 Education Through Innovation and Entrepreneurship* ($5k), and the *Innovation in Social Educational Entrepreneurship* (I-SEE) ($30k).

University Technology Transfer Functions

Arizona Technology Enterprises (AzTE)[xvi] is the technology venture arm of Arizona State University. In addition to ASU technologies, AzTE also manages technologies developed by ASU's partner universities, Dublin City University in Ireland (through its technology commercialization organization, Invent DCU Limited) and Tec de Monterrey in Mexico. AzTE is located at SkySong and works in collaboration with ASU's *Innovation and Entrepreneurship* to bolster these relationships. AzTE collaborates with each university to protect and commercialize their intellectual property in the United States.

ASU also has a number of activities focused on student entrepreneurship, global company attraction, and investor network development. The addition of technology transfer to international collaborations increases the likelihood that global discoveries will be commercialized utilizing Arizona networks. Over time, ASU's development of vibrant global networks is expected to positively impact economic development in the State.

- Among U.S. institutions with at least $200 million in research expenditures, AzTE ranked in the top ten for invention disclosures, licenses and options, and startups formed per $10 million in research.
- ASU faculty submitted a record 187 invention disclosures in the fiscal year 2010. ASU expects these inventions will provide the technology inventory for the next generation of new deals or startups .

University-Industry Collaboration

The Sensor, Signal and Information Processing Center and Consortium (SenSIP) at ASU has been designated a National Science Foundation (NSF) Industry/University Collaborative Research Center. The consortium researchers have provided the mathematical and algorithmic groundwork for technology used in security systems, consumer electronics, medicine health care, nanotechnology, and other technologies including global positioning systems.

The Aerospace and Defense Research Collaboratory, a consortium between ASU, UA and Embry-Riddle Aeronautical University, is intended to bridge the gap between education and industry through research. The Collaboratory is housed on ASU's Polytechnic campus in the College of Technology and Innovation.

- This research initiative is expected to boost Arizona's economy, as well as attract other big corporations to the state.

ASU's Biodesign Institute[xvii] in collaboration with industry is engaged in a $5 million, four-year project to identify protein biomarkers that could predict cardiovascular disease in people with type 2 diabetes. The collaboration is sponsored by the *National Institute of Diabetes and Digestive and Kidney Diseases* (NIDDK--part of the National Institutes of Health). Other collaborators in the project include *Pfizer* and the *Phoenix VA Healthcare System*. The money comes from a fund that is designed to support scientists from different disciplines to work together on a common problem.

Other ASU industry collaborations include: Adaptive Intelligent Materials and Systems Center (AIMS); Advanced Technology Innovation Center; Arizona Institute for Nano-Electronics (AINE), and the Arizona State University Research Park.

Regional and Local Economic Development

ASU's unique assets – including intellectual capital, advanced facilities and student talent – are invaluable in developing a regional economic ecosystem where innovation-based firms can thrive. As a regional economic engine, ASU injects revenue back into the community through student, visitor, and staff spending, and by providing a stable source of employment for thousands of Arizonans.

More specifically, ASU provides the following economic impact in the regional and local economic development[xviii]:

- *ASU directly employs* over 20,000 Arizonans, generating $961 million in wages;
- *Spending by visitors to ASU or sponsored events* generated $69 million;
- *ASU student spending* directly generates $248 million of labor income in the state of Arizona;
- *ASU employee and student spending* pumps over $1.8 billion into the local economy every year; and
- *Arizona taxpayers invest* $386 million a year in ASU, and realize a $3.4 billion economic yield on their investment.

Deep-Dive Questions

- Is innovation an integral part of ASU's institutional culture?
- Why is it important? And how does it influence entrepreneurship and tech transfer?
- How do you envision your program in the future?
- What is your vision for each of the case study's bucket, especially regional and local economic impact?
- How does your institution leverage (or intend to leverage) geographic endowment?
- Are your innovation, entrepreneurship, and tech transfer programs integrated?
  – Why, or why not?

- How has ASU's one university in many places (multiple campus & online) model hindered or helped faculty and student innovation?
- Are there any unique successes (and or challenges) you may wish to highlight?

Conclusion

Mr. James O'Brien's comments have been instructive in better understanding ASU's leadership role in promoting innovation, entrepreneurship, and the commercialization of research in the nation's universities, in addition to the impact of the NACIE commitment letter in framing ASU's strategic plans and institutional culture.

The Office of Innovation and Entrepreneurship thanks ASU's assistance with this case study, and looks forward to a continued close and collaborative relationship in building America's innovation infrastructure.

Entrepreneurship, Innovation, and Commercialization of Research at the Georgia Institute of Technology

Overview – A Focus on Industry and Collaboration[24]

The Georgia Institute of Technology (Georgia Tech), a public research university in Atlanta, Georgia, is part of the University System of Georgia. Established in the 1880s on the heels of the Industrial Revolution, Georgia Tech's mission has always focused on assisting industry. For example, the university's basic and applied research efforts have been instrumental for the global aerospace industry, with Georgia Tech scientists playing key roles in the development of radar and other flight technologies. Georgia Tech focuses intently on the basic-to-applied research continuum throughout its comprehensive research programs in engineering, physical and life sciences, computing, and policy. Georgia Tech's Strategic Vision and Plan[xix] infuses a focus on innovation and entrepreneurism across the spectrum of basic and applied research as well as in its educational programs. Viewed in broad themes, research at Georgia Tech includes work in:

- Big Data;
- Biotechnology and Biomedicine;

[24] Comments by Jilda D. Garton, Vice Provost for Research, General Manager, GTRC and GTARC

- Electronics and Nanotechnology;
- Manufacturing, Trade, and Logistics;
- Materials;
- National Security;
- Paper and Science Technology;
- People and Technology;
- Public Service, Leadership, and Policy;
- Robotics;
- Sustainable Infrastructure and Energy; and
- Systems.

Georgia Tech's culture embodies a collaborative approach. It enlists outside partners and contributors including academic, governmental, industry, and nonprofit institutions in an effort to better understand and ensure the benefit of research to the nation. In 1937, Georgia Tech established what is now the Georgia Tech Research Corporation (GTRC), an internal outpost for engineering experimentation and entrepreneurial applications of engineering, science, and technology. Georgia Tech also operates the oldest and largest university-based business incubator in the United States, the Advanced Technology Development Center, which was established in the 1980s to provide a range of services and facilities for entrepreneurs to launch and build new companies. Recognized by Forbes in 2010[xx], the Advanced Technology Development Center has graduated 143 new companies, which have helped create millions of dollars in revenues and which together have attracted nearly $2.5 billion in capital activity. Capital activity includes venture capital funding, other investment, and the value of mergers and acquisitions.

Georgia Tech incorporates several strategies to ensure that it continually improves and expands its services to industry. To ensure it meets its fiduciary responsibilities and maintains public trust and confidence, the university continually strives to reduce bureaucratic barriers and modify underperforming initiatives. For example, the university has launched the Georgia Tech Integrated Program for Startups, GT:IPSTM, which combines a streamlined licensing program with organized support for faculty and student inventor-entrepreneurs. The program provides information and education for entrepreneurs to help them form stronger, more successful companies, and the streamlined GT:IPS license agreement helps simplify negotiations and "take the drama off the table."

Three of Georgia Tech's more recent initiatives to promote innovation and entrepreneurship based on broad stakeholder partnerships include Flashpoint,

NSF I-Corps, and the Global Center for Medical Innovation. Flashpoint, a Georgia Tech startup accelerator program established in 2011, encourages basic and applied research and facilitates their transfer to the marketplace through entrepreneurial education and access to experienced mentors, experts, investors, and stars in an open, immersive, shared-learning workspace.

In July 2012, Georgia Tech was named as a node for the National Science Foundation's I-Corps program. former NSF Director Subra Suresh described I-Corps as a program to "leverage productive public-private partnerships and extend the impact of fundamental research discoveries." He noted that it has "inspired the research and business communities to collaborate in new ways." Georgia Tech is serving as a teaching site for the hands-on I-Corps curriculum.

Finally, the Global Center for Medical Innovation, which opened in 2012 with support from the Economic Development Authority's i6 Program, will bring together core members of the medical device community — including universities, research centers, clinicians, established device and drug companies, investors, and early-stage companies — with the goal of accelerating the commercialization of innovative medical technology.

The NACIE commitment letter was broadly disseminated to Georgia Tech faculty and administrators and elicited general consensus prior to President Peterson's endorsement. University stakeholders who were invited to review and comment on the letter were found to be already committed to its expressed ideas and goals. The letter's real impact was to add "force" and "intentionality" to Georgia Tech's innovation, entrepreneurship, and tech transfer strategic vision by providing a time scale for faculty and administration efforts, documenting their commitment, and holding them accountable.

Innovation and entrepreneurism are hallmarks of educational programs as well as research and technology transfer. Problem-based learning gives students an opportunity to develop ideas and technologies within their disciplines, and increasingly, activities such as the General Electric Smart Grid Challenge[xxi] provide a venue for companies to explore disruptive concepts through student engagement.

Below is an enumeration of several Georgia Tech programs and initiatives that support the five buckets in the NACIE sponsored university commitment letter.

Student Entrepreneurship

Students at Georgia Tech are an active part of research and discovery. In fact, over 70 percent of invention disclosures name one or more students among the inventors. As part of a broader effort to foster innovation and entrepreneurship within its student community, Georgia Tech has several initiatives, including:

- **Georgia Tech Integrated Program for Startups, GT:IPS** — An initiative that supports faculty and student inventor-entrepreneurs through two components: *GT:IPS Facilitation*, a graduated program of support, information, and education for new company founders; and ***GT:IPS License***, which offers the same terms to all Georgia Tech startups in the same field and provides them with transparency into Georgia Tech Research Corporation's (GTRC) licensing processes.
- **InVentureTM Prize**[xxii] — An annual competition that inspires undergraduate teams to create inventions that will be judged by experts for more than $30,000 in cash prizes from Georgia Tech and sponsoring corporations. First and second place winners receive patent filings funded by GTRC, and in March 2011, a "People's Choice" award was sponsored by NCR Corporation.
- **TI:GER** — An award-winning program and partnership between Georgia Tech and Emory University School of Law that brings together PhD, MBA, and law students to experience the challenges of commercializing innovative technologies. Now approaching its 10th anniversary in 2012, TI:GER is expanding to global entrepreneurship and has become an established part of the entrepreneurial education of graduate students on both campuses.
- **Business Plan Competition** — An annual competition, now in its 11th year, held by the Scheller College of Business and the Institute for Leadership and Entrepreneurship to foster entrepreneurship among Georgia Tech students and recent alumni. Since its inception, more than 650 participants have received approximately $570,000 in cash and services, and each year several teams launch companies to take their product concepts to market. To date, eight winning teams have been accepted into Georgia Tech's Advanced Technology Development Center.
- **Ideas to SERVE (I2S)** — An annual competition of ideas where creativity, imagination, and the use of technology are applied innovatively to solve community and social issues and sustain the environment. Started as a specialty track of the Business Plan Competition in 2009, I2S has quickly grown into a separate event, contributing to Georgia Tech's portfolio of programs that foster

entrepreneurship. I2S is open to Georgia Tech students and recent alumni.

Faculty Entrepreneurship

Georgia Tech has several awards and programs to incentivize faculty to mentor graduate students, or themselves, to pursue innovative research and entrepreneurial ideas. These include:

- **Bio-impact Commercialization Team (BCT)**[xxi] — An initiative focusing on research in biomedicine whereby faculty members and the venture capital community work closely with experts in the biomedical device space to facilitate translational research and commercialization. The Wallace H. Coulter Foundation will fund the BCT's translational research and development projects.
- **The Georgia Tech Fund for Innovation in Research and Education (GT FIRE)** — A program that facilitates planning for large extramural proposals — those of strategic value to the Institute that have more than $500,000 in direct costs per year—and provides support for feasibility studies of transformative ideas in research and/or education. This past spring, faculty submitted 42 transformative proposals, from which three research-related ideas and four education-related ideas were selected for funding.

University Technology Transfer Functions

- **The Georgia Tech Research Corporation (GTRC)** — The contracting entity responsible for several of the university's tech transfer and licensing processes. GTRC also aims to accelerate the formation of robust Georgia Tech spinout companies and broaden participation in entrepreneurship among faculty and students. In addition, GTRC has revised master agreement terms and developed new template agreements to meet the needs of industry sponsors as technologies progress in development.
- **Georgia Tech VentureLab** — A one-stop-shop providing comprehensive assistance to faculty, research staff, and graduate students who want to take their technology innovations from the laboratory to the commercial market. VentureLab specialists help these innovators "start up" by assisting in business plan development, connecting them with experienced entrepreneurs, and locating sources of early-stage financing, including seed grants from the Georgia

Research Alliance. The program has fostered, on average, one new spinout each month over the last three years.

- **Georgia Tech Edison Fund** — A source for modest investments into early-stage technology startups that have a strong connection to Georgia Tech. This fund makes use of targeted charitable contributions from Georgia Tech alumni and friends.

University-Industry Collaboration

- **University-Industry Demonstration Partnership (UIDP)** — An activity of the National Academies that works to demonstrate innovative approaches to research engagement and improve relationships with private industry for research and commercialization of inventions. Georgia Tech has been a member and active participant since the UIDP was founded in 2005. The recently published Researcher Guide, a collaborative effort of UIDP university and industry members, provides information for university and company scientists and engineers who wish to engage in sponsored or collaborative research.
- **The Office of Industry Collaborations and Affiliated Licenses (ICAL)**[xxiii] — An organization that works in close coordination with faculty, academic units, and university offices, including the Office of Sponsored Programs, Office of Innovation Commercialization and Translational Research, Enterprise Innovation Institute (EI^2), and Advanced Technology Development Center, in their partnerships with private industry to help promote industry-sponsored research and further technology commercialization. Types of agreements facilitated by ICAL include nondisclosure, industry collaboration, consortium, memorandum of understanding, center bylaws, testing, and SBIR.

Regional and Local Economic Development

An economic impact study by the Selig Center for Economic Growth at the University of Georgia's Terry College of Business[xxiv] indicates that Georgia Tech made a $2.3 billion economic impact during the fiscal year 2011, the highest of any institution in the University System of Georgia (USG).

The study also found that Georgia Tech generated 18,640 full- and part-time jobs. Most of the economic impact in the study consists of initial spending by USG institutions for salaries and benefits, supplies and expenses, and other budgeted expenditures, as well as spending by students who attend the institutions.

Georgia Tech also impacts the local and regional economy in several others ways, including:

- Research partnerships with business and industry in the state of Georgia and throughout the Southeast;[xxv]
- Economic development services to help make Georgia's small and medium-sized businesses and communities more innovative and efficient;
- The more than 48,000 Georgia Tech alumni who live and work in the state;
- Research labs that produce more than 300 invention disclosures annually;
- A strong patent portfolio, ranked eighth among the top 124 universities according to the 2009 Universities Patent Scorecard ;
- Spinning off an average of ten new companies a year;
- The Economic Development Authority i6 grant, which Georgia Tech received in 2010 to support innovation and entrepreneurship and boost the quality of high-growth startups in the region. EDA funding has helped advance economic development activities through Georgia Tech's University Center of Excellence and also through a recent Jobs Accelerator award, where Georgia Tech partners with Gwinnett Tech to prepare students for work in health information technology; and
- EI^2, which serves Georgia through a network of industry specialists located in nine regions throughout the state. These specialists provide local businesses with direct technical and engineering assistance, professional education courses, networking opportunities, and connections to Georgia Tech resources.

During fiscal year 2011 alone, Georgia Tech's Enterprise Innovation Institute (EI^2):

- Evaluated 219 Georgia Tech innovations and helped form 17 new companies based on this intellectual property, which attracted nearly $100 million in investment;
- Helped manufacturing companies reduce operating costs by $35 million, increase sales by $191 million, and create or save 950 jobs through the Georgia Manufacturing Extension Partnership program, a

program funded by the National Institute of Standards and Technology Manufacturing Extension Partnership, the state of Georgia, and industry clients;
- Assisted 493 start-up technology companies through the Advanced Technology Development Center. These companies attracted nearly $100 million in venture capital investment and mergers/acquisitions; and
- Helped Georgia companies win $492 million in government contracts, creating an estimated 9,843 jobs through the Georgia Tech Procurement Assistance Center.

Deep-Dive Questions

- Is innovation an integral part of Georgia Tech's institutional culture?
- Why is it important? And how does it influence entrepreneurship and tech transfer?
- How do you envision your program in the future?
- What is your vision for each of the case study's buckets?
- How does your institution leverage (or intend to leverage) geographic endowment?
- Are your innovation, entrepreneurship, and tech transfer programs integrated? – Why, or why not?
- Are there any unique successes (and or challenges) you may wish to highlight?

Conclusion

The Georgia Institute of Technology is a top-10 public research university and an Association of American Universities (AAU) member school. Jilda Garton's comments have been instructive in better understanding Georgia Tech's many entrepreneurship, research, and technology transfer programs, in addition to the impact of the NACIE commitment letter in framing Georgia Tech's strategic plans and institutional culture.

The Office of Innovation and Entrepreneurship thanks Georgia Tech's assistance with this case study and looks forward to a continued close and collaborative relationship in building America's innovation infrastructure.

Entrepreneurship, Innovation, & Commercialization of Research at Howard University in Washington, DC

Overview – Making the Commitment[25]

Howard University is a federally chartered, non-profit, private, co-educational and historically black university located in Washington, D.C. It has a Carnegie Classification of Institutions of Higher Education status of RU/H: Research Universities, which signifies high research activity.

The President of Howard University is Dr. Sidney A. Ribeau, and the Dean of the Business School is Barron H. Harvey, Ph.D. Dr Harvey, who is a member of the National Advisory Council on Innovation and Entrepreneurship (NACIE) and is a major advocate for the innovation, entrepreneurship, and commercialization programs at Howard.

As a comprehensive, research-oriented university, Howard's mission is to provide a high quality educational experience at a reasonable cost to people of both genders and all races. In addition to the undergraduate program, Howard has several graduate schools and colleges. Howard's business school facilitates several entrepreneurship programs and competitions, while several technology based initiatives are managed by the science schools and colleges.

Howard has many of the foundational pieces that are necessary to realize its innovation and commercialization potential. The university is a member of the National Nanotechnology Infrastructure Network (NNIN), an integrated partnership of fourteen user facilities that is supported by National Science Foundation (NSF). Howard's research lab provides opportunities for nanoscience and nanotechnology research. The Howard Nanoscale Science and Engineering Facility (HNF) facilitates research and development in diverse areas including electronics, materials science, optics, polymer science, membrane technology, medicine, physics and chemistry.

NNIN laboratories including Howard's HNF have been accessed by over 6,000 users, and over 1,500 small companies use the facility as incubator; this has been resulting in the spinoff of several small companies. Academic users, such as university faculty and students who primarily use the facility for research, are charged a nominal fee. Corporate fees are marginally higher, and the relatively small fee negates the need for price discrimination between large and small firms. Companies may also permanently station staffers at the lab, without losing full rights to their research and development (R&D). Many

---

[25] Comments by: Barron Harvey, Ph.D., Dean, Howard University School of Business; Gary Harris, Ph.D., Director, Howard University Nanoscale Science and Engineering Facility (HNF); and John Gloster, J.D., Senior Associate General Counsel, Howard University.

federally funded facilities are now modeled after the National Nanotechnology Infrastructure Network.

The Small Business Innovation Research (SBIR) affiliated businesses are encouraged by Howard to conduct their Federal Research/Research and Development (R/R&D) activities at HNF. Student involvement is encouraged either through individual projects or partnerships with faculty and HNF corporate clients. This model of a "shared research lab facility" represents a cultural shift, especially for typically sheltered corporate research. Paradoxically, scarce and increasingly competitive research grants and high equipment costs are barriers that have been fostering this collaborative culture. Even so, hiccups remain. Despite being in operation for decades, the lab - just like many others around the country - is not yet self-sustaining.

These hiccups are not limited to HNF facilities. Several entrepreneurship programs and competitions at Howard's Business School may be shrunk or eliminated due to limited funding. Consequently, the evolved philosophy at Howard is to build a staple of research that would interest industry. A professional outside party now has marketing responsibilities for research outputs, and outside counsel has been retained to handle patent filings for the Tech Transfer Office.

Howard University intends to establish a culture of entrepreneurship throughout the university and considers OIE's outreach an affirmation of on-going innovation and entrepreneurship advocacy within the university. However, uncertainty over the long-term prospect of several innovation and entrepreneurship programs suggests that Howard's chances of reaching its innovation potential will be better enhanced by unequivocal, strong, and consistent support by the university president and his leadership team. The foundations of innovation and entrepreneurship are present; they now require a strong commitment by the president and his team.

Below is an enumeration of Howard University programs and initiatives that support the five buckets in the NACIE sponsored university commitment letter.

Student Entrepreneurship

Howard University was one of eight institutions selected by *the Ewing Marion Kauffman Foundation* in a nationwide competition to receive a multi-million dollar grant as part of the *Kauffman Campuses Initiative* to develop an entrepreneurial climate across college campuses in America. The program seeks to transform the way entrepreneurship is taught and experienced so that any student, regardless of their field of study, will have the opportunity to participate.

The Entrepreneurship, Leadership and Innovation Institute (ELI) was thus created, with matching support from Howard University and other partners. ELI seeks to provide the skills, tools and orientation required for entrepreneurial development and success in the African-American and minority communities with particular emphasis on providing educational opportunities for all stakeholders. The ELI's Executive Director is Ms. Johnetta Boseman Hardy, and she has oversight of the following initiatives:

- *Entrepreneurship at Howard* actively counsels and mentors students with ideas for new businesses, or seeking assistance in improving their business model
- Each month, the ELI Institute features a student start-up at Howard University
    - Featured start-ups are ventures that are innovative, have participated in the bi-weekly *BlackMarketplace,* or have had considerable growth in clientele, sales, or visibility on-campus or in the Washington, DC Metropolitan Area
- *Black Market Place* showcases businesses owned by Howard students, alumni, faculty, and staff
- *Entrepreneur of the Year* is an ELI Institute award given to prominent and exceptional on-campus entrepreneurs. The award recognizes Howard students who have built impactful and worthwhile business ventures, excelled in academics, and exhibited a meaningful dedication to the community at-large through service.
- *Annual Business Plan Competition*[xxvi] is an ELI Institute co-sponsored business plan competition for Howard University students. The top 4 winners receive cash prizes. First place winner(s) receive $10,000, second place winner(s) receive $6,500, third place winner(s) receive $3,000, and lastly an Award for Special Presentation of $500.
- *Concept 120*[xxvii] is a business plan contest held each semester that emphasizes the elevator pitch. Students develop their ideas and sales pitch as if they were in front of a potential investor or business client – the bulk of the contest depends on the contestants' ability to sell an idea.
- *The StartUp Scramble DC University Challenge*[xxvii] brings entrepreneurially-minded college students from DC universities

together for a weekend-long event to build and launch sustainable ventures that address social issues affecting local communities

- ELI Institute offers an array of academic programs for the studentsxviii
    - Undergraduate non-business majors can elect to minor in entrepreneurship;
    - Graduate students can elect to concentrate in entrepreneurship; and
    - All students are able to gain a certificate in entrepreneurship.

In addition to current students, ELI Institute contributes to the entrepreneurial success of many Howard University alums including Ike C. Nwaneri, one of the two co-founders of *KEADWORKS LLC*[xxix] and *KOJAMI Inc*[xxx].

Keadworks is a creative marketing and technology agency in the Washington DC Metro Area which has launched successful campaigns for various industry clients.

Kojami Inc. is a company spawned out of Keadworks LLC to provide the following electronic services: It is an events platform that has been widely adopted by event organizers, businesses and organizations especially in the Washington metro region

- The platform allows both individual and corporate event organizers to create an event in 3 minutes or less and easily manage and track multiple elements of the event in one simple dashboard;
- Scheduled events can then be easily propagated through mobile phones as a mobile application—recipients of the mobile event can also interact and SHOVE (share) the mobile event; and
- Recipients can also complete a one-touch GPS navigation search, view and join conversations of each event in real-time, purchase and receive mobile tickets and most importantly stay connected to the category of events desired.

Kojami in many ways is re-inventing the way people use mobile devices to create, manage, interact or share (SHOVE) events.

Faculty Entrepreneurship

The ELI Institute also specializes in faculty training, and serves which enhance their role as repository for a wide range of internal and external research. Additionally, ELI Institute's Lecture Series, Annual Conference on Entrepreneurship, and Fund for Academic Excellence spearheads innovation in teaching entrepreneurship, and documenting trends.

ELI Institute features two dedicated research directions for faculty[xxxi]:

1. Black Entrepreneurship and Business Development—Designed to explore African-American, Caribbean, and African entrepreneurial models and approaches; and
2. African-American/Urban Demographics—Identifies key trends in the community's purchasing power and habits that shape this trillion-dollar market. As well as explore ways for African-A merican business to derive value from these trends.

The ELI Center for Research provides a national forum for learning about African-American entrepreneurs and entrepreneurial ventures. The Center for Research will:

- Provide fellowships for faculty, students, and other scholars to engage in fundamental and practical research on entrepreneurship as it relates to the African-American community (through fellowships and grants);
- Publish a research journal, case studies, and white papers;
- Host an annual symposium and conduct several conferences on critical research topics;
- Create a clearinghouse for valuable data and information about African-American entrepreneurs, market opportunities, and business development trends; and
- HBCU Faculty Conference on Entrepreneurship will advise Howard University faculty and their HBCU colleagues on methods to introduce concepts of entrepreneurship into their courses, while also assuming leadership roles in infusing such thinking into the broader curriculum on their campuses.

In addition to the ELI Center, *The Research Administration Services*[xxxii] facilitates and administers interdisciplinary research capacity growth and indirect cost recovery at Howard University. This includes integrated education and research strategies, professional development, and internal controls of sponsored activities.

University Technology Transfer Functions

The Intellectual Property Center[xxxiii] is the central technology transfer resource for Howard University researchers, inventors and investors. While Howard University Trademarks works to promote, enhance and elevate the image of Howard University by authorizing the use of the university's name and logos on merchandise, Howard University requires that all individuals, organizations, departments and companies -both internal and external - obtain prior approval before using any Howard indicia.

Notable inventions from research conducted at Howard University include[xxxiv]:

- **Nanotechnology - Industrial Lubricants:** Metal Forming Fluids with Dispersed Nanoparticles for Improved Lubrication, by Mosleh, Mohsen, Ph.D. et al.
- **Electrical Engineering, Lighting Systems, LED Array Control:** Localized Distributed Control Method of LED Lighting Array and its Fixture, by Kim, Charles, Ph.D.; NS
- **Chemical Engineering, Clean Coal, Coal:** Process for Removal of Hazardous Air Pollutants from Coal, by Aluko, Mobolaji, Ph.D., et al.

Additionally, the Intellectual Property Center manages research outputs from several Howard University Institutions, these include:

- The Howard Nanoscale Science and Engineering Facility (HNF) and The Howard University Cancer Center;
- The Howard University Center for Sickle Cell Disease and Center for Energy Systems and Controls (CESaC);
- The NOAA Center for Atmospheric Sciences (NCAS) and The Center for Drug Abuse Research (CDAR);
- The Institute for Multimedia Applications (IMA) and The Collaborative Alcohol Research Center (CARC);
- The Capstone Institute; and The Center for Pre-Professional Education;
- The Center for Urban Progress (CUP) and The Howard University District of Columbia Small Business Development Center (DCSBDC); and
- The National Minority AIDS Education and Training Center (NMAETC); and The Howard University Research Administration.

University-Industry Collaboration

Howard University is an educational outreach partner of the *Smart Lighting Engineering Research Center*[xxxv]. The Center develops new technologies and applications that will change the way society uses lighting. Beyond illumination, Smart Lighting Systems will simultaneously provide high speed data access and scan for biological and biochemical hazards.

- More than 40 faculty members from multiple institutions with diverse backgrounds and disciplines work together in teams on the Center's research programs.
- Constant contact with industrial and scientific advisory boards ensures projects are relevant, and work output is benchmarked to insure they are cutting edge.

Howard University has also partnered with the Center for Applied High Performance Computing *(CAHPC)*[xxxvi] on a project that applies data fusion to make supercomputing applications easy to use.

Howard University is also a participating member of *the Power Systems Engineering Research Center (PSERC)*[xxxvii], a university-industry collaboration focusing on research and education needs in the electric power industry.

- The Industrial Advisory Board (IAB), composed of PSERC industry members, meets twice per year with PSERC researchers and students to conduct Center business, and engage in discussions about the Center's research and education activities.

The Georgetown-Howard Universities Center for Clinical and Translational Science (GHUCCTS) is a private industry-backed cooperative between the two universities. *Bridgeline Digital, Inc.*, developer of the award-winning iAPPS web experience management (WEM) platform and interactive technology solutions, launched a new comprehensive website developed to support medical research collaboration between Georgetown and Howard Universities[xxxviii]. GHUCCTS seeks to advance public health by performing research that has positive impact on human health and well-being.

Regional and Local Economic Development

The Georgia Avenue, Development, Growth, and Enterprise Transformation Center (GADGET Center)[xxxix] at *Howard University School of*

Business is located on Georgia Avenue, and staffed by graduate students and counselors from the *DC SBDC at Howard University*. GADGET provides free consulting services to local businesses and will focus on growth and development of the commercial district adjacent to Howard University.

More broadly, the District of Columbia Small Business Development Center Network (DC SBDC), an outreach program of Howard University, has joined forces with the U.S. Small Business Administration (SBA), other District of Columbia universities, and community organizations. This collaborative provides free management, technical assistance, and affordable training in all phases of business development to small businesses based in the District of Columbia[xl].

DC SBDC provides confidential, one-on-one management assistance at no cost to DC-based small businesses and aspiring entrepreneurs. Business consulting services include but are not limited to cash flow analysis, financial forecasting, market research, procurement assistance, proposal cost analysis, overall business assessment "the business health checkup," startup feasibility analysis, business plan assessments, strategic planning and business start-up information.

In addition to the above mentioned initiatives, Howard University also confers a Minor in Community Development[xli] which is an interdisciplinary program intended to provide students with the knowledge, tools, and practical experience to play a proactive role in community revitalization in cities throughout the world.

Howard University also plays an integral role in neighborhood revitalization initiatives. As an example, it partnered with the Washington, D.C., government, Fannie Mae, and other corporations to transform 45 abandoned, university-owned properties in a crime-ridden neighborhood into more than 300 housing units and $65 million in commercial development[xlii].

Additionally, in 2010[xliii] Howard University had a workforce totaling 6,934 full—and part—time employees (excluding students) of which approximately 28 percent (based on payroll disbursements) resided in the District of Columbia representing an annual payroll of $103.8 million. Howard University also made an estimated $94.5 million in non-payroll expenditures for goods and services to vendors and contractors located within the District. As previously indicated, Howard University undertakes capital projects that employ DC-based contractors and workers who reside in the City. Combined, payroll and non-payroll in 2010 within the District of Columbia totaled $198.3 million.

Deep-Dive Questions

- Is innovation an integral part of Howard's institutional culture?
- Why is it important? And how does it influence entrepreneurship and tech transfer?
- How do you envision your program in the future?
- What is your vision for each of the case study's bucket, especially regional and local economic impact?
- How does your institution leverage (or intend to leverage) geographic endowment?
- Are your innovation, entrepreneurship, and tech transfer programs integrated?
  – Why, or why not?
- Are there any unique successes (and or challenges) you may wish to highlight?

Conclusion

Howard University continues to outperform many HBCU universities in several critical categories and recognition. It is, for example, the only HBCU University classified as a RU/H: Research Universities (high research activity) by Carnegie's Classification of Institutions of Higher Education.

Howard University also appears to leverage its Washington, D.C. location to attract public and private funding. Howard is a private university which also enjoys partial funding by the U.S. Department of Education to the tune of $235 million annually. The Ewing Marion Kauffman Foundation, through its Kauffman Campuses Initiative, is also a major funder of several Howard University entrepreneurship and innovation initiatives.

Howard University appears to be on the cusp of realizing its potential. However the University's leadership must now make a commitment to institute and promote cohesive innovation and entrepreneurship programs, and institutional culture. And there is reason for optimism; The Dean of Howard University School of Business, Barron H. Harvey, Ph.D., is a member of the National Advisory Council on Innovation and Entrepreneurship (NACIE). Dr. Harvey is also a tireless advocate for the innovation, entrepreneurship, and commercialization programs at Howard.

Comments by Dr. Harvey and his colleagues have been instructive in better understanding Howard's various innovative entrepreneurship, research and technology transfer programs, as well as understanding the impact of the NACIE commitment letter in framing Howard's strategic plans and institutional culture.

The Office of Innovation and Entrepreneurship thanks Howard University's assistance with this case study, and looks forward to a continued close and collaborative relationship in building America's innovation infrastructure.

Entrepreneurship, Innovation, & Commercialization of Research at Lorain County Community College in Elyria, Lorain County, Ohio

Overview – Innovative First Among Equals[26]

Lorain County Community College (LCCC) is a public, open-access community college located in Lorain County, Ohio. In this way, it is just one of perhaps thousands of community colleges in the United States; in truth, LCCC has differentiated its self from the pack in several innovative ways to become a unique and arguably first among equals community college.

LCCC is the only community college in Ohio that offers a University Partnership. This partnership enables students to earn bachelors' and masters' degrees from any of eight Ohio universities without leaving the LCCC campus[xliv]. LCCC is also the first college in the state of Ohio to build an advanced technologies center for business and industry. Consequently, all LCCC students now have access to the Fab Lab[xlv], which is aligned with MIT.

LCCC's Fab Lab is based on the concepts of Dr Neil Gershenfeld, the director of the Massachusetts Institute of Technology's Center for Bits and Atoms. A Fab Lab is a collection of commercially available machines that can be used to "make just about anything with features bigger than those of a computer chip." Realistically, it offers the tools needed to "conceptualize, design, develop, fabricate and test" a wide variety of things[xlvi].

Lorain County Community College President is Dr. Roy A. Church, who is credited with leading the effort to develop a regional University Partnership to improve local access to education by offering more than 40 bachelor and master degree programs from 8 area colleges and universities on LCCC's campus. This unique initiative eventually led to the formation of the *Innovation Alliance* between LCCC and the University of Akron.

LCCC's innovative entrepreneurship and commercialization initiatives have also been duly recognized. President Obama has visited the school twice,

---

[26] Many of the comments are culled from LCCC Proud: http://www.lcccproud.com/ community /dr-roy-a-church-of-lorain-county-communitycollege-to-receive-h-peter-burg-regional-vision-award

and the college enjoys federal government support for some of its critical programs. Even so, to realize its commitment to the National Association for Community College Entrepreneurship (NACCE), LCCC has adopted strategies which include the five buckets in the NACIE-sponsored university commitment letter.

Below is an enumeration of LCCC programs and initiatives which support the five buckets in the NACIE sponsored university commitment letter.

Student Entrepreneurship

As part of the *Entrepreneurship Experiential Education Program*[xlvii], businesses that receive Innovation Fund (IF) grants are provided opportunities for students, faculty and staff to experience firsthand what it's like to be an entrepreneur. This educational component is a unique feature of the IF funding process.

LCCC also offers the following academic programs, clubs and resources to better prepare students for an entrepreneurial career:

Educational Opportunities

- Innovation Fund Education Experience;
- Associate of Applied Business - Entrepreneurship; and
- Certificate in Entrepreneurship.

The Students in Free Enterprise Club is open to all students who are interested in exploring careers in the business world. The club's programs and activities include guest speaker series, seminars, and company tours.

LCCC also provides the following electronic resources to aid student entrepreneurship:

- **Entrepreneur.com**—features Information to Help Start, Grow, and Manage A Small Business;
- **Entrepreneur Assist**—Free Tools and Services for Your Business;
- **Inc.com**—The Daily Resource for Entrepreneurs; and
- **Fast Company**—Where Ideas and People Meet.

In addition to programs and clubs, LCCC has several academic programs to quip students become entrepreneurs or become highly skilled employees at innovative companies. These academic programs include:

- **Alternative Energy Technology—Wind Turbine program**[xlviii] in LCCC is the first associate's degree credit program in wind power in Ohio.
- Graduates enter the job market as wind turbine technicians trained to construct and repair turbine units.
- A one-year certificate of proficiency program is also available, helping displaced workers get retrained quickly and back into the workforce.

The Materials Joining Institute–Welding Technology program confers an associate's degree, a one-year technical certificate, or a short-term certificate in welding technology. This training prepares graduates for the welding profession which projects a 250,000 deficit in skilled workers in the coming years (American Welding Society).

Faculty Entrepreneurship

The Innovation Fund of the LCCC Foundation makes grants to technology business "start-ups" who in return provide opportunities for students, faculty and staff to experience firsthand what it's like to be an entrepreneur[xlix].

As a direct benefit of this program, LCCC encourages faculty to incorporate entrepreneurism into course curriculums, regardless of its topic or field of study, because the whole notion of entrepreneurism is critical in any work environment today.

Faculty may elect to structure entrepreneurship experiential learning opportunities for students as a practicum or independent study.

- Faculty should seek to give students projects that deliver a highly-focus work-based learning goals combined with theoretical coursework.

Practicum or independent project may include:

- Completing a marketing or business plan;
- Performing research for an entrepreneurial employer; and
- Developing a survey or performing market research.

University Technology Transfer Functions

LCCC does not have a traditional technology transfer office. However, LCCC is a major contributor to coalitions that facilitate technology transfer, and in some cases creation of technological processes, that positively impacts the region's economy.

In its partnership with **NorTech—the Northeast Ohio Technology Coalition**—LCCC has taken a leading role in fostering the development of new technology in Northeast Ohio. The coalition focuses on the industries of advanced materials, power, information and communication technology, bioscience and health care, and electronics. NorTech builds on the strengths of the region and propels new technology-based industries into the global economy.

University-Industry Collaboration

Advanced Manufacturing Careers—LCCC is one of four community colleges selected nationally to pilot the *National Association of Manufacturers* (NAM)-endorsed *Manufacturing Skills Certification System*[l].

The NAM-endorsed Skills Certification System focuses on the core, basic skills required for entry-level workers in all sectors of manufacturing, from alternative energy and computers to aerospace and life-saving pharmaceuticals. The skills certifications address personal effectiveness competencies, foundational academic competencies, general workplace skills and manufacturing industry-wide technical skills. Entry-level science, technology, engineering and math (STEM) skills are included in the system.

The Bill & Melinda Gates Foundation awarded a $1.5-million grant to the Manufacturing Institute (MI) to comprehensively plan and implement post-secondary education programs that include the National Association of Manufacturers (NAM)-endorsed Manufacturing Skills Certification System.

Weld-Ed—the National Center for Welding Education and Training[li], headquartered in LCCC, through its Weld-Ed program develops national curriculum and trains welding educators and technicians. From repairing underwater structures to welding in outer space, Weld-Ed trains students for a value-added welding career.

LCCC is a member of the *Manufacturing Advocacy & Growth Network* (MAGNET), a regional collaboration of manufacturers, educational institutions, economic organizations and chambers of commerce.

- Partners work together to champion manufacturing technologies by assisting manufacturers with all aspects of the industry.
- MAGNET also advocates for manufacturers with local and regional regulatory agencies.

Regional and Local Economic Development

The Innovation Alliance[lii] between LCCC and the University of Akron accelerates education efficiency, knowledge creation, and economic development across all sectors vital to the success of the Northeast Ohio region.

The Alternative Energy degree is collaborative between LCCC, Stark State Community College, Lakeland Community College, and Cuyahoga Community College that leverages program sharing as a way to save costs and offer diverse educational programs to more students.

The Innovation Fund is a regional fund that supports early stage entrepreneurial endeavors and emerging technology based companies located throughout Northeast Ohio. It is administered through a network of regional and state higher education, government and economic development partners. The Fund is operated from within the LCCC Foundation and enhanced by the Great Lakes Innovation and Development Enterprise (GLIDE). To date more than $3 million has been awarded to 44 companies who have generated over $25 million of additional investment and revenue growth.

On February 22, 2011, the White House endorsed the launch of: *Innovation Fund America*, modeled after LCCC's the *Innovation Fund*[liii].

Deep-Dive Questions

- Is innovation an integral part of LCCC's institutional culture?
- Why is it important? And how does it influence entrepreneurship and tech transfer?
- How do you envision your program in the future?
- What is your vision for each of the case study's bucket, especially regional and local economic impact?
- How does your institution leverage (or intend to leverage) geographic endowment?
- Are your innovation, entrepreneurship, and tech transfer programs integrated?
  – Why, or why not?
- Are there any unique successes (and or challenges) you may wish to highlight?

Conclusion

Lorain County Community College (LCCC) has earned a reputation as an innovation center due to its various programs and national and regional recognitions. The president of the United States has visited the campus and also instituted a national innovation program that draws inspiration from LCCC Innovation Fund. LCCC has also built innovative alliances with other academic institutions, industry, and industry associations.

Alliances with other universities allow students to earn 4-year degrees on LCCC campus. Industry and industry association collaborations has deepened the quality of technical degree and certificate programs offered to LCCC students.

While LCCC is not a signatory to the NACIE commitment letter, it has been no less instructive to learn about the impact of the NACIE commitment letter in framing LCCC's strategic plans and institutional culture.

The Office of Innovation and Entrepreneurship thanks Lorain County Community College's innovation and entrepreneurship initiatives, and looks forward to a close and collaborative relationship in building America's innovation infrastructure.

Entrepreneurship, Innovation, & Commercialization of Research at the University of Michigan at Ann Arbor, Michigan

Overview—Leadership & Advocacy

The University of Michigan and its president, Dr. Mary Sue Coleman, have played leadership and advocacy roles in promoting innovation and research commercialization at the nation's universities. The university has prioritized innovation and entrepreneurship's role in economic development prior to the development of the NACIE commitment letter; for the last several years, major strategic priorities for the University of Michigan include stimulating economic development and growth in Michigan and beyond through innovation and entrepreneurship.

President Coleman's decision to spearhead the NACIE commitment letter is a natural extension of the innovation and commercialization culture at U-M. Even so, the NACIE Letter has had a "*conscious raising*" effect on the innovative culture at U-M. Innovation and commercialization is a key focus of the activities of the president, executive officers, faculty, and staff at U-M. The outcome of this focus is reflected in the expanding array of programs, policies, relationships, and activities aimed at spurring innovation and entrepreneurship on campus, in the region, and across the nation. As part of U-M's strategy, many aspects of this commitment are highlighted regularly in university outreach and communications, ranging from speeches by senior executives to a central website accessible from the university's home page.

U-M has also constituted a Communications Team to articulate a comprehensive strategy for these various innovation and commercialization initiatives. The team includes the Vice President for Research, the VP for Communications, the senior government relations officer, and Mr. David Lampe, Executive Director of Research Communications, in the Office of the Vice President for Research. Mr. Lampe is also charged with coordinating all efforts related to innovation and entrepreneurship at U-M.

The "*Innovate!*" website is part of this broader strategy for a unified outlet that captures various innovative programs at the business, engineering, and law schools. Another unique outcome of U-M's innovation culture is that patents and licensing have become an explicit part of tenure and promotion considerations.

President Coleman's various engagements also underscore U-M's strategy of promoting research commercialization through collaborative public- and private-sector relationships. President Coleman currently serves as chair of the *Association of American Universities*, and the *Internet2 Board of Trustees*. President Obama selected her as one of six university presidents to help launch *the Advanced Manufacturing Partnership*, a national effort bringing together industry, universities and the federal government. And in 2010, President Coleman was named co-chair of the *National Advisory Council on Innovation and Entrepreneurship.*

U-M faculty and staff are also engaged in university association initiatives, as part of a sustained effort to better communicate the economic impact of universities. This includes Mr. David Lampe co-Chairmanship of APLU's Strategic Communications and Advancement Working Group.

Other collaborative U-M relationships include the *Ann Arbor SPARK*, a non-profit created to position the Ann Arbor region as a prime destination for innovative businesses. Ann Arbor SPARK also accelerates the development of startups, supports the growth of established businesses, and connects businesses with relevant talent. Another collaborative relationship is with the *Michigan Economic Development Corporation* (MEDC), a public-private partnership serving as the state's marketing arm and lead agency for business development and economic growth. Among other services, MEDC provides capital programs for businesses, strategic partnerships, talent enhancement, as well as urban and community development.

The University Research Corridor (URC) is a partnership between U-M, Michigan State University, and Wayne State University. The Research Corridor leverages the intellectual capital of member schools to spark regional economic development. The URC achieves its mission through entrepreneurship, innovation and technology transfer programs, educating a work force prepared for the knowledge economy, and attracting smart and talented people to the state of Michigan.

In addition to partnerships and advocacy, U-M has also learnt a very informative lesson about requirements for a successful commercialization program; a strong commitment by the university president and leadership is invaluable. Especially as the president's bully pulpit is a powerful tool that motivates, informs, and excites the community into action. Successfully engaged communities are force multipliers. Successful programs understand this and build on the institution's character. These programs let a thousand flowers bloom, rather than allow hierarchy to stifle innovation. These programs set priorities, and then hammer away at them repeatedly. These program characteristics position the school as a driver of economic development.

Below is an enumeration of University of Michigan programs and initiatives that support the five buckets in the NACIE sponsored university commitment letter.

Student Entrepreneurship

Through its tradition of action-based, interdisciplinary learning, the University of Michigan primes its students to be tomorrow's most innovative business leaders. Michigan graduates are entrepreneurs in the truest sense and have fueled the formation of many industry-leading businesses from technology startups to some of the world's leading companies including Google, Domino's Pizza, Sun Microsystems, Stryker Corp., H&R Block, Borders, and Federal Express.

- The U-M College of Engineering and the Ross School of Business has created a joint *Michigan Master of Entrepreneurship (MsE) degree*. The MsE program, which will admit its first class in the fall of 2012, will educate students on forming and managing high-growth potential, scalable businesses.
- A *minor in entrepreneurship*, available to students from across the university, is also under development.

At present, there is a wide range of non-degree programs across all curricula, including:

- The *Zell Lurie Institute for Entrepreneurial Studies*, at the Ross School of Business, engages undergraduate and graduate students in real world learning. Launched in 1999, the Institute has granted over $2.3 million to student start-ups. In addition to spearheading efforts to spread entrepreneurship across campus by introducing multidisciplinary courses, hosting university-wide business-plan competitions and grant programs, it has spawned entrepreneurship centers at the Law School, Medical School and College of Engineering.
- The *Center for Entrepreneurship* (CFE), in the College of Engineering, offers entrepreneurship-related undergraduate courses, a nine-credit *Program in Entrepreneurship* (PIE) where both undergraduate and graduate students from U-M may earn a certificate of completion, and a 15-credit *CASE in Entrepreneurship* (CASEE) where graduate students, as well as working professionals, are taught the fundamental tools necessary for bringing innovative ideas to market. Since its inception 2,830 students have enrolled in CFE sponsored classes.
- *Zell Entrepreneurship and Law Program* (ZEAL), at the U-M Law School, prepares law students to advise and/or develop business enterprises and has established a clinic providing much sought-after legal services for student entrepreneurs in university programs.
- *Medical Innovation Center* (MIC), in the U-M Medical School, assists faculty, alumni and partners in taking ideas through the early development stage toward commercialization. Established in 2008, the Center offers a fellowship program in biomedical innovation and also operates a Design and Prototype Lab. The first cohort of fellows launched a medical device company before its fellowship year had ended.
- The *Center for Venture Capital & Private Equity Finance* (CVP), at the Ross School of Business, offers a specialized focus on entrepreneurial finance and investment through research and program initiatives. Established in 1994, Center initiatives such as the annual Michigan Growth Capital Symposium and Private Equity Conference effectively connect the University's entrepreneurial network to the broader financial community. These programs are administered through the Zell Lurie Institute.

Other Student-Focused Activities Include the Following

- CFE and ZLI jointly manage the U-M *TechArb Student Accelerator*. With the aid of an advisory board of community leaders and professional investors and additional funding from the Office of the Vice President for Research, TechArb helps early stage companies founded by U-M students refine and develop their ideas and business plans, and eventually showcase teams to funders.
- *MPowered Entrepreneurship* is a student group created and run by students to expose their fellow students to entrepreneurship and support student ventures through coordinated events and network. MPowered sponsors several high-profile activities to encourage student involvement, notably the 1,000 Pitches campaign, a campus-wide idea competition, the MPowered Career Fair, focused on growth companies, the Ann Arbor Startup Weekend, to connect students with the local startup community, and eRes, a living and learning entrepreneurial student community.
- *Tech Start program* is an 8-12 week full time summer internship overseen by U-M Tech Transfer for graduate students from many academic areas including Law, Engineering, Medicine, Business and Information Technology, offers participants an intensive experience working on entrepreneurial projects.
- *Entrepreneurial Multidisciplinary Action Projects* (EMAP) offered by the Ross School of Business/Zell Lurie Institute for Entrepreneurial Studies immerses student teams in domestic and international entrepreneurial businesses to execute assignments that may include developing business plans, identifying new product opportunities or formulating market entry strategies. EMAP projects are required of all first year business graduate students.
- *Three student-run Venture Funds*—the $5.5 million early stage *Wolverine Venture Fund*, the five-year-old pre-seed *Frankel Commercialization Fund*, and the first student-run *Social Venture Fund*— a new initiative to support emerging businesses.
- The *Marcel Gani Internship program* places students at start-up and venture capital firms.
- The *Dare to Dream grant program* leads students through a six-month thoroughly mentored process that enables them to explore an idea, establish feasibility and launch a venture. Based at the Ross Business School, the program was expanded in 2007 to non-business students under a partnership with the Center for Entrepreneurship in

the College of Engineering. Support ranges from $500 to $10,000. In 2010 almost $90,000 in total was awarded.

- *Michigan Business Challenge* is a four-phase campus-wide business plan competition that selects four finalists to compete for top prizes with over $60,000 awarded throughout the cycle. The Ross Business School operates and funds the competition which attracted 73 teams in 2010. Ambiq Micro, the 2010 winner, has already attracted significant venture capital.
- *Course projects* provided by U-M Tech Transfer for classes such as Finance 629 (Financing Research Commercialization) at the Ross School of Business and the Master's in Entrepreneurship program, as well as investment analysis and consideration by the Wolverine Venture Fund and the Frankel Commercialization Fund managed by the Zell Lurie Institute for Entrepreneurial Studies.
- *Entrepreneurial and legal mentoring services* provided by U-M Tech Transfer to student projects within the Center for Entrepreneurship, the Zell Lurie Institute for Entrepreneurial Studies and other entrepreneurial units across campus.
- *Tech Transfer Fellows program* through which graduate students under the supervision of Tech Transfer professionals provide written initial assessments of the commercial aspects of newly reported inventions.
- The *Entrepreneur and Venture Club* (EVC) at the Ross School of Business brings together students dedicated to furthering their education and professional goals as prospective entrepreneurs and investors in new ventures. The EVC provides events, networking opportunities, and educational programs to provide students with the skills and contacts to advance their ambitions.
- *SI Create* is a student organization fostering a community of innovation and entrepreneurship at the U-M School of Information. The club sponsors field trips that expose students to innovation and hosts a Business Model Competition.
- *The China Entrepreneur Network* (CEN) is aimed at building a global hub for Chinese Entrepreneurs. The U-M is host to both a campus-wide club and a business school student club. CEN also organizes a yearly conference with worldwide participants.
- *The Society for Business Engineers*, at the College of Engineering, supports students in the Engineering school with an interest in

applying to programs in other areas of study as well as obtaining an entrepreneurship certificate

- *Entrepalooza* is an annual conference that introduces students to successful entrepreneurs through presentations and a "lunch and learn" where they can meet one-on-one with seasoned entrepreneurs and investors.
- *TedXUofM* is a student group that sets up an annual innovation conference with a 2000+ audience and large web-presence.
- *Student Trips* to high profile companies allowing them to network with entrepreneurs, venture capitalists and U-M alumni entrepreneurs are organized by the Center for Entrepreneurship to the San Francisco Bay area, New York and Chicago.
- *Entrepreneurship Hour* invites distinguished innovators to campus every week to share their stories. The speaker series is a class taught through the Center for Entrepreneurship and is open to the public. The talks are also recorded and made available online.

Tech Fest is an annual program launched in 2011 that welcomes entrepreneurs, venture capitalists, angel investors, scientists and business leaders from around the world to campus for demonstrations of labs and student projects, networking and brainstorming.

Faculty Entrepreneurship

The University of Michigan has several incentives to encourage faculty to pursue innovative and entrepreneurial ideas and to mentor graduate students to do so. It also helps to nurture the success of companies based on technology developed at U-M. These incentives include:

- The Provost has encouraged *recognition of innovation and entrepreneurship in faculty tenure and promotion* cases. He specifically cites working with U-M Tech Transfer to patent or license and invention; launching a start-up company; and encouraging or instructing students in entrepreneurial activities.
- The *U-M Venture Center* within *U-M Tech Transfer* provides a one-stop hub for faculty entrepreneurs as well as investors looking for start-up opportunities based on U-M research.
- The *Venture Accelerator* provides state-of-the-art laboratories, equipment, and offices for emerging U-M companies from the

pipeline of U-M start-ups, as part of a full suite of services and resources from the *U-M Venture Center.*

- Under the *Michigan Investment in New Technology Startups Program*, U-M invests up to $1 million of university funds in start-ups based on U-M technology, after they have secured initial funding from a qualified venture capital firm.
- The *U-M Distinguished University Innovator Award* recognizes the faculty's important and lasting contributions to the economy by moving new innovations into the private sector for public benefit, and by demonstrating entrepreneurial success.
- The *U-M Tech Transfer Ted Doan Award for Outstanding Leadership in Entrepreneurship and Innovation* is awarded to a deserving individual who has demonstrated a distinguished record of encouraging entrepreneurship and innovation for the state of Michigan.
- The *U-M Tech Transfer annual inventor recognition reception, Celebrate Invention*, honors faculty who participate in tech transfer activities amidst a celebration with over 300 business, venture, university and community partners.

U-M also invests in infrastructure to support innovation and entrepreneurship. The *North Campus Research Complex*, a two million square foot array of office and laboratory space, was acquired in 2009. Formerly a Pfizer R&D center contiguous with the campus, the complex houses a variety of the university's innovation and entrepreneurship activities, including:

- Space for interdisciplinary teams of U-M faculty to come together to conduct translational research in such areas as health policy, biointerfaces, cardiovascular research, and translational oncology
- U-M Tech Transfer, the Venture Center, and the Venture Accelerator;
- The Business Engagement Center, which develops and manages relationships with industry partners; and
- Facilities for U-M research partners, including biopharmaceutical spinoff Lycera Corp. and Boropharm, a chemical development and manufacturing business

University Technology Transfer Functions

The Office of Technology Transfer (OTT) at U-M oversees the commercialization of new technologies and research discoveries, and provides professional resources for inventors, entrepreneurs and industry partners. It is the university's conduit between laboratory research and corporate commercialization interests[liv].

U -M Tech Transfer utilizes several resources to connect entrepreneurs and other members of the business and venture communities to opportunities at U-M. These include[lv]:

- A highly proficient team of *Licensing Specialists* provide inventors and business partners with responsive technology assessment, patenting services, market analysis and contracting services;
- *Tech Transfer Fellows* employs mentored graduate and post-doc students to assist U-M Tech Transfer licensing specialists in providing comprehensive technology assessments;
- *Catalyst*, a talent resource network that connects entrepreneurs and other parties with U-M's technology and venture opportunities;
- *The Venture Center* employs a team of experienced entrepreneurs in its *Mentors-inResidence* program to assist in connecting technology and start-up projects to other entrepreneurs, businesses and venture partners;
- The Center also leverages relationships with over 250 premier venture capital firms and angel groups to assist entrepreneurs engaged with U-M opportunities; and
- *U-M Tech Transfer* and the *Office of Research and Sponsored Programs* lower the barriers to industry investment in university research by offering sponsors the opportunity to negotiate the terms for licensing possible intellectual property during the initial contracting process.

These and various other initiatives have helped accelerate the launching of several ventures, placing U-M among the top 10 universities in the nation in spin-off activity and technology licensing.

- *93 start-up ventures* from 2001 to 2010, many of which have had notable market success such as HealthMedia, HandyLab, Arbor Networks and Accuri Cytometers.
- Creation of *814 agreements* from 2001 to 2010, connecting U-M technology with entrepreneurs in new and existing companies.

- With *101 licensing agreements* and the spin-off of *11 startups* in 2011, U-M consistently ranks in the top 10 U.S. universities in tech transfer performance.

Some other University activities assisting U-M Tech Transfer include:

- *"Gap" funds* from the proceeds of U-M Tech Transfer central administration revenues, matched by State-funded programs, are used to address key commercialization issues. These gap funds are deployed in concert with "translational research" investments from the College of Engineering (CoE), the CoE Coulter process, Office of the Vice President for Research funds and a planned Medical School fund.
- *The Michigan Growth Capital Symposium* is a venture capital event that connects high potential Midwest start-ups and university spin-outs with leading investors nationwide. Ten year statistics include: 300 companies presented; 200 raised capital totaling more than $1.7 billion; 60 exited successfully.
- *College of Engineering Technology Development Fund* offers awards of up to $50,000 to later-stage research activities related to translational research proof of concept
- *Coulter Foundation Translational Research Fund* provides translational funding to 4-8 new biomedical engineering projects a year at up to $100,000 per project
- *The Michigan Institute for Clinical and Health Research (MICHR) Pilot Grant Program* awards $50,000 to $250,000 for bench to bedside and bedside to practice translational research.

University-Industry Collaboration

The *Business Engagement Center* (BEC),[lvi] affiliated with the Office of the Vice President for Research and the Office of University Development, provides companies with a one-stop gateway to the various research, technology, education, facilities, and talent resources at U-M. The BEC maintains affiliated offices in the College of Engineering, the Medical School, and at the Dearborn and Flint campuses. Founded in 2007, the BEC now maintains relationships with more than 1,000 companies, and is contacted by nearly 200 new companies each year.

The BEC-facilitated relationships can range from individual research projects to broader engagements, depending on the business need. For example, aerospace giant Boeing maintains a long-standing partnership with U-M focused on building a pipeline for the future. Boeing recruits from seven different U-M programs, provides support for 50 students, regularly sponsors student projects, and conducts research with four different departments.

One of the functions of the BEC is to work with schools and departments to encourage industry sponsorship of research at U-M. Total sponsorship reached $61.6 million in FY 2011.

Some research initiatives are emerging that specifically aim to spur innovation and economic development in partnership with industry and government. *The Michigan Sustainable Transportation Imperative* is an emerging initiative that aims to bring U-M's interdisciplinary strengths together with representatives from the transportation and related industries as well as state and federal government agencies to strengthen the state's leadership in the next generation of transportation vehicles and systems.

U-M also maintains close relationships with its 450,000 member alumni network and engages a number of U-M alumni in businesses, venture firms and other organizations around the world. Some examples include:

- *Larry Page*, co-founder and CEO of search engine giant *Google*, earned a B.S. degree in engineering with a concentration in computer science from U-M in 1995. *Google AdWords* has an office in Ann Arbor
- *Eric Lefkosfsky* and *Brad Keywell*, founders and founding investors in *Groupon*. Both earned undergraduate degrees in 1991 and Law School degrees in 1993 from U-M. Lefkofsky founded a business while still a U-M undergrad
- *Thomas Bumol,* VP Biotechnology and Autoimmunity Research for Eli Lilly in San Diego, CA, earned a B.S. degree in microbiology from U-M in 1975. Tom sits on the U-M Tech Transfer National Advisory Board;
- *Bill Joy*, co-founder of Sun Microsystems, earned a bachelor's degree in computer engineering in 1975. He currently is a partner in the venture firm *Kleiner Perkins Caufield & Byer's Green Tech Practice*;
- *Tony Fadell*, a key initiator of the *iPhone and the iPad products at Apple,* started three companies before graduating from U-M with a bachelor's degree in computer engineering in 1991; and
- *John Denniston* is a partner in Kleiner Perkins Caufield & Byers, a leading venture capital firm. John has a B.A in Economics and a J.D.

from U-M and also serves on the U-M Tech Transfer National Advisory Board.

Regional and Local Economic Development

U-M and its senior management team provide "thought leadership" on America's economic development policy. Examples include:

- *President Mary Sue Coleman* was appointed a founding co-chair of the *National Advisory Council on Innovation and Entrepreneurship*, created by the U.S. Department of Commerce in 2010 to support President Obama's innovation strategy by helping to develop policies that foster entrepreneurship and technology transfer;
- *Vice President for Research Stephen Forrest chaired Ann Arbor SPARK*, the Ann Arbor region's economic development organization from 2009 to 2012; and
- As an institution, U-M was selected as one of six universities to collaborate in a new national *Advanced Manufacturing Initiative* recommended by President Obama's *Council of Advisors on Science and Technology.*

The *University Research Corridor* (URC) is a consortium among U-M, Michigan State University, and Wayne State University. This effort was undertaken to highlight the capabilities and impact of the state's three leading research institutions and drive the transformation of Michigan's economy. Among its activities, the URC produces an annual economic impact report that includes an assessment of the impact of the three universities on a different industry sector each year. Some impact figures:

- The URC economic impact on Michigan increased from $12.9 billion in 2006 to $15.2 billion in 2010;
- URC spends more than $1.8 billion in research, and educates 137,583 students;
- More than 573,000 URC alumni live in Michigan, earning $28.6 billion in 2010, which is 16.4 percent of all wage and salary income in the state;
- The URC generated $426 million in 2010 state tax revenue even as state support for higher education has declined; and
- The URC averages 135 patents per year (140 in 2010) and has spun off an average of 14 companies per year since 2006.

U-M has also provided leadership on three innovative partnerships with other Michigan universities, funded by the Michigan Economic Development Corporation:

- The *Michigan Corporate Relations Network* (MCRN) is a statewide university network designed to create partnerships that will connect Michigan's corporations to critical university assets to help promote innovative research and grow Michigan's economy. Six major public universities in Michigan make up the network.
- The *Tech Transfer Talent Network* is a collaborative network among 7 universities led by the University of Michigan to establish regional talent tools, programs and resources to enhance university tech transfer performance. Modeled after several U-M tools and programs, the Talent Network provides funds for regional and shared resources to enhance the commercialization of university research.
- The *Michigan Initiative for Innovation and Entrepreneurship* (MIIE) and the *Michigan Universities Commercialization Initiative* (MUCI) are statewide collaborations among public universities to promote regional economic development and entrepreneurship.

U-M's *Institute for Labor, Employment, and the Economy* has programs aimed at assessing, understanding and encouraging economic development. They include:

- The *Center for Business Acceleration and Incubation Studies*, which carries out market feasibility studies for proposed new business incubators in the region to help lay the foundation for success.
- The *Technology Commercialization and Assistance* program proactively identifies the capabilities and initiatives of emerging or established companies and matches them with technology available at Michigan universities.
- The *Accelerate Michigan Innovation Competition,* an international business plan competition initiated in 2010 highlights Michigan as avenue for innovation and opportunity. The competition, one of the largest of its kind, is sponsored by a network of groups in Michigan committed to bolstering innovation and entrepreneurship in the state. U-M co-sponsors the event through the University Research Corridor. Four U-M ventures have won prizes.

Deep-Dive Questions

- Is innovation an integral part of U-M's institutional culture?
- Why is it important? And how does it influence entrepreneurship and tech transfer?
- How do you envision your program in the future?
- What is your vision for each of the case study's bucket?
- How does your institution leverage (or intend to leverage) geographic endowment?
- Are your innovation, entrepreneurship, and tech transfer programs integrated? – Why, or why not?
- Are there any unique successes (and or challenges) you may wish to highlight?

Conclusion[lvii]

Across U-M, more than *1,500 students* participated in the *more than 100 courses* offered at U-M related to entrepreneurship. *More than 5,000 students* participated in entrepreneurship activities in 2010-11, in classes, competitions, public events and more. One survey showed more than 15 percent of incoming freshmen had started a business before enrolling.

In addition to investments in human capital, U-M also continues to invest in infrastructure. The *North Campus Research Complex*, a two million square foot array of office and laboratory space, was acquired in 2009. The complex, formerly a Pfizer R&D center, houses the Venture Accelerator and serves as a locus for many of the university's economic development efforts.

Beyond investments in human capital and infrastructure, U-M also continues to align its bureaucratic structure to fully leverage regional endowments. The *Business Engagement Center*, the *Medical School Business Development* team and the *College of Engineering's Corporate Relations* office now collectively serve as the front door to businesses seeking to identify and access U-M resources. Together, these offices manage more than 1,000 active relationships with companies ranging from entrepreneurial start-ups to Fortune 500 enterprises. Separately, the *U-M Medical School Business Development team* connects faculty with external collaborators and helps both navigate the most efficient path to accelerate research from "bench."

Lastly, Mr. David Lampe's comments have been instructive in better understanding U-M's leadership role in promoting innovation, entrepreneurship, and the commercialization of research in the nation's universities. As well as the impact of the NACIE commitment letter in framing University of Michigan's strategic plans and institutional culture.

The Office of Innovation and Entrepreneurship thanks U-M's assistance with this case study, and looks forward to a continued close and collaborative relationship in building America's innovation infrastructure.

Entrepreneurship, Innovation, & Commercialization of Research at the University of North Carolina at Chapel Hill

Overview – University of the People[27]

The University of North Carolina (UNC) at Chapel Hill is an original member of "The Triangle," a group of three universities—North Carolina State University, Duke University, University of North Carolina at Chapel Hill—whose research facilities and the educated workforce they provide have historically served as a major attraction for businesses located in and around the region, which came to be known in the 1950s as the Research Triangle Park (RTP) in North Carolina.

Currently, the entrepreneurship program at UNC, Chapel Hill was driven by former Chancellor Holden Thorp, an academician, NACIE member, former entrepreneur and venture capitalist, who has co-written a book, Engines of Innovation, about innovation on university campuses[lvii]. Even so, the UNC Chapel Hill community believes that what sets their school apart from others is that "it is, as it was meant to be, the University of the people[lix]".

The "University of the People" ethos also extends to the current structure of the entrepreneurship programs at UNC, Chapel Hill. Entrepreneurship has moved from the exclusive domains of the business and engineering schools to the people, as the university moves to institutionalize a campus-wide culture of entrepreneurship.

Along with the students, the faculty is also encouraged to think entrepreneurially. An invitation only faculty boot camp sponsored by the Chancellor affords 20 faculty members (at a time) the opportunity to develop their business ideas. Support services include assistance with business plans and workshops. Students are also given opportunities to translate their entrepreneurial plans into viable commercial ventures.

The Center for Entrepreneurial Studies[lxi] at the Kenan-Flagler Business School is UNC Chapel Hill's flagship entrepreneurial program. The Center

[27] Comments by Judith Cone, Special Assistant to the Chancellor for Innovation & Entrepreneurship at University of North Carolina at Chapel Hill

offers staff, faculty, and especially students the resources to identify and evaluate valuable entrepreneurial opportunities.

The Office of Technology Development (OTD)[lix] is UNC, Chapel Hill's technology transfer office. OTD advances UNC, Chapel Hill's mission to encourage innovation and disseminate knowledge. Principally, the OTD serves the UNC Chapel Hill community and the public by licensing innovations developed by faculty, students and staff.

In addition to encouraging university wide entrepreneurial culture, UNC, Chapel Hill believes there is still a strong role for the government in promoting innovation and commercialization at the nation's universities. This role includes increasing funding for proof-of-concept centers, instituting further patent reform, and revising immigration law to make it easier for American companies to hire bright American university trained immigrant students.

UNC, Chapel Hill also welcome and value OIE's deep dives on university innovation and commercialization. And to realize its commitment to the five buckets in the NACIE sponsored university innovation and commercialization letter, UNC, Chapel Hill has adopted the following strategies:

Student Entrepreneurship

With over 20 MBA electives, the entrepreneurship curriculum at Kenan-Flagler covers a broad spectrum, including specialty topics such as family business, entrepreneurship through acquisition, and social entrepreneurship.

In addition, the Center for Entrepreneurial Studies boasts a wide range of programs, conferences and competitions which deeply enrich the entrepreneurial experience of, and allow students to engage their entrepreneurial interests through a variety of perspectives. These include:

Programs, Conferences, & Competitions

Startups[lxii]

- *Launching the Venture* is a series of courses that help faculty, staff and students from across the UNC campus turn new ideas into viable ventures
    - The mission of the program is to equip aspiring UNC entrepreneurs with the tools to successfully launch their venture;
    - MBA students may explore ventures of their own or join teams as "free agents";

  - The Launch curriculum comprises four distinct phases: Opportunity, Feasibility, Business Planning and Financing; and
  - Launch teams undergo weekly coaching sessions in which they receive invaluable feedback from successful entrepreneurs and domain leaders.

  Outcomes
  - Since its inception in 1999, Launch has aided in the creation of 50 startups.
- *The Carolina Challenge* is an annual startup competition open to all UNC students, staff, faculty, and alumni
  - Entrants compete in one of four tracks: *traditional, social, high tech and scientific*
  - Entrants undergo several rounds of competition, including an elevator pitch round
  - Activities surrounding the Carolina Challenge span the academic year, including a campus-wide idea competition in the fall

  Outcomes
  - The Carolina Challenge awards $50K in prize money each year.
- *The Venture Capital Investment Competition* (VCIC) gives MBA student teams the unique opportunity to learn about venture funding by acting as venture capitalists and evaluating the viability of five real startup ventures.
  - *VCIC's 40 events* have become a network of mini-venture fairs in which MBAs and Venture Capitalists (VC) get an early peek at viable startups.

  Outcomes
  - VCIC competition now attracts *1,200 students, 150 venture capitalists and 100 entrepreneurs* each year from three different continents; and
  - 1/4 of aspiring entrepreneurs in VCIC mini-venture fairs go on to raise venture funding.
- *Student-Run Private Equity Fund: The Kenan-Flagler Private Equity Fund* which launched in 2007 is the first and only student-run fund associated with a top-tier global business school that seeks to provide real returns to its limited partners
- Kenan-Flagler also boasts two student-run real estate funds and a fund dedicated to investing in publically-traded companies
  - The private equity fund management team comprises nine Kenan-Flagler students, five second-year MBAs and four BSBAs

- All students serve a three-semester term with the program
- In addition to active investment activities, students participate in a series of private equity courses, lectures and events
- Students manage all aspects of the investment cycle: raising capital, sourcing deals, performing due diligence, making investment decisions and presenting decisions to the Board of Directors.

Outcomes

- The Kenan-Flagler student run Private Equity Fund now has more than $4.4 million of committed capital under management; and
- ZCapital Partners and James J.Zenni awarded a $100,000 grantto the Kenan-Flagler BusinessSchooltosupportprivateequity(PE) educationforMBAand undergraduate business students[lxiii].

Faculty Entrepreneurship

Former Chancellor Thorp's co-author, Buck Goldstein is the University Entrepreneur in Residence and Professor of the Practice in the Department of Economics. Mr. Goldstein is the co-founder of *Information America*, an online information and database business, which evolved over a 15-year period, from start-up through venture financing to public company. Information America was eventually acquired by the Thomson Corporation. Mr. Goldstein subsequently became a partner in Mellon Ventures, the venture capital arm of Mellon Bank, where he served on the Board of numerous early stage information companies[lxiii].

In addition to Mr. Goldstein, many practicing entrepreneurs, venture capitalists, venture lawyers and others who have the most current and relevant knowledge on specific entrepreneurial topics also teach entrepreneurship courses[lxiv].

Faculty members are encouraged to and recognized for exemplary faculty scholarship. Faculty recognition initiatives include:

- *The C. Felix Harvey Award* is given to the UNC faculty member or members whose proposed outreach project best reflects applied innovation of scholarly expertise in the humanities and social sciences. It seeks to support faculty who want to move their research findings from the campus to directly serve communities.
- *Launch the Venture*[lxv] is an interactive 6-month course designed to assist faculty entrepreneurs in evaluating the feasibility of their potential company, designing a business strategy and creating a

business plan. The course is free to UNC-affiliated faculty, staff and students. It is offered by the Office of Technology Development (OTD) in partnership with the Kenan-Flagler Business School.

University Technology Transfer Functions[lxvi]

OTD typically handles approximately 125 novel technologies yearly, generating over 50 patent filings, 30 license agreements and 3-5 startup companies.

- OTD's services include evaluating, patenting, licensing and assisting faculty in obtaining research support from corporate sponsors.
- OTD serves to fulfill UNC Chapel Hill's mission to advance knowledge, enhance education, and solve societal problems, and enrich the quality of life in the State of North Carolina by:
    - Facilitating the translation of new discoveries into useful products
    - Attracting industry research collaboration; and
    - Stimulating local and regional economic development.
- OTD's professional project managers have considerable expertise in science, business development, and intellectual property law. OTD provides the following services when UNC-Chapel Hill faculty, staff, and students report their innovations:
    - Evaluate the innovation for commercial potential;
    - Take steps to obtain appropriate protection for the intellectual property represented by the innovation;
    - Identify strong prospects for commercial partnership; and
    - Negotiate appropriate licensing agreement(s).
- OTD's licensing activities also includes copyright works and trademarks, a variety of programs to license and disseminate software, multimedia and tangible research property for both research and commercial applications
- OTD also develops, reviews and negotiates Material Transfer Agreements to facilitate the movement of research materials to and from the University

OTD Internship and Fellowships

- The OTD internship program is an eight month position for graduate students and/or post-doctoral fellows who wish to learn more about intellectual property and technology commercialization

    - The internship runs during the academic year, from August to May, and requires a commitment of approximately 8-12 hours per week.
    - Interns will participate in a formal training series covering the basics of technology transfer, conduct market assessments and direct marketing efforts for select technologies, and gain exposure to ongoing negotiations between OTD and industry partners.
- *OTD Training Series* include a monthly series of internal training sessions for interns, new OTD employees and visiting technology transfer professionals.
- *OTD Market Analyses* is a critical initiative that includes performing market assessments of promising UNC technology.
- *Gillings Innovation Labs* focuses on solving significant public health challenges with fundamental breakthroughs in public health, through competitively funded research programs.
    - The Gillings School of Global Public Health established a $50 million fund with a gift from Dennis and Joan Gillings to anticipate emerging public health challenges, accelerate solutions, and improve people's lives across the state and the world.

University-Industry Collaboration

UNC Chapel Hill maintains several collaborative relationships with industry groups to enhance industry access to their research expertise, intellectual property, and commercial opportunities. These include:

- *The Council for Entrepreneurial Development* (CED)[lxvii] members have a shared mission to identify, enable and promote high-growth, high-impact companies and to accelerate the entrepreneurial culture of the Research Triangle and North Carolina. CED members are a community of people inspired by entrepreneurship. They include startup companies, more mature growth-stage firms, investors, service partners, academics, and individuals.
- *North Carolina Biotechnology Center*[lxviii] provides long-term economic and societal benefits through support of biotechnology research, business, education and strategic policy by:
    - Serving as the statewide hub of life-science commercialization;
    - Bootstrapping companies and new business sectors with loans and other support;

  - Funding key faculty recruitment and commercially promising research;
  - Linking academic, business, civic and policy leaders;
  - Supporting workforce development activities; and
  - Providing curriculum development and workshops for educators.
- *North Carolina Small Business Technology Development Center* (SBTDC)[lxix] is a program of The University of North Carolina System, in partnership with the U.S. Small Business Administration, which provides resources for growing and developing businesses. These resources include: Training & Education for Business Startups; Direct Service to Economic Development Organizations, Government Agencies, and University Departments; and Leverage University Resources Statewide.
- *North Carolina Innovative Development for Economic Advancement* (NC I.D.E.A)[lxx] provides small grants to high-tech startup companies to support business activities that validate potential markets, reduce risk of early failure, and advance projects to the point of self-sustainability at which time they are suitable for private equity investment.

Internships and Fellowships programs are another collaborative vehicle between UNC, Chapel Hill and industry. These programs include:

- *The Carolina Entrepreneurial Fellows Program* (CEF) is a collaborative effort between the Center and the MBA Entrepreneurship Club which matches entrepreneurial students with local startups
  - Typically students work two days a week with one startup (perhaps their own), two days at another startup and each Friday on group projects.
  - This 2/2/1 format gives students a broad entrepreneurial experience and exposure to the local startup community.
  - Internships are funded by clients, the *MBA Entrepreneurship Club* and the N*orth Carolina Small Business Technology and Development Center.*
- *The Carolina Venture Fellows Program* (CVF) is inspired in part by the *Kauffman Fellows Program*. CVF is a highly competitive program that places select students in a structured twelve-month apprenticeship with a venture capital firm

- The venture fellow works part-time during the school year and full-time during the summer.
- Over twelve months, the venture fellow is involved in all facets of a venture firm: sourcing deals, structuring investments, assisting portfolio companies and fundraising

Outcomes

- Venture firms that have participated in CVF include: Intersouth Partners, IDEA Fund Partners, Southern Capitol Ventures, A.M. Pappas&Associates, SJFVentures, Hatteras Venture Partners, Parish Capital, Golden Pine Ventures, Dogwood Equity, The Aurora Funds and Carrboro Capital

- *The Alternative Investments Fellows Program* (AIF) connects MBAs with rare summer internship opportunities at private equity and hedge funds
  - These internships allow students to be involved in all facets of the firm's investment process, including: sourcing deals, due diligence, valuing and structuring investments, and assisting portfolio companies
  - Proceeds from the *Alternative Investments Conference* help fund the fellowships.

Outcomes

- Participating firms include: Brown Brothers Harriman, North State Capital Investors, Bank of America Global Strategic Capital, The Halifax Group, Jacobs Capital, and Google.

Regional and Local Economic Development

UNC Chapel Hill participates in several economic development initiatives that impact the regional economy. These include:

Innovate@Carolina: Important Ideas for a Better World[lxxi] has raised more than $11 million for a new $125 million fundraising campaign developed by UNC alumni and friends experienced in leading innovation in science, business, medicine, nonprofits and academia to bring the power of innovation and entrepreneurship to bear on the world's biggest problems.

Outcomes

- UNC's membership in a consortium created by a $3.6 million gift from the Blackstone Charitable Foundation .
- The consortium will help the Research Triangle develop a network of entrepreneurial assistance similar to those in Silicon Valley and the Boston Corridor.

- Partners include Duke University, North Carolina State University, North Carolina Central University, and the Center for Entrepreneurial Development.

Impact (anticipated)

- The network has the potential over a decade to create jobs, attract seed, startup and expansion capital, and generate revenue

Deep-Dive Questions

- Is innovation an integral part of UNC Chapel Hill's institutional culture?
- Why is it important? And how does it influence entrepreneurship and tech transfer?
- How do you envision your program in the future?
- What is your vision for each of the case study's bucket?
- How does your institution leverage (or intend to leverage) geographic endowment?
- Are your entrepreneurship and tech transfer programs integrated?
  – Why, or why not?
- Are there any unique successes (and or challenges) you may wish to highlight?

Conclusion

UNC Chapel Hill appears to have on-going initiatives in all areas of its commitment to initiate and expand technology commercialization processes, encourage entrepreneurship, and institute policies and programs that support regional economic development. However, there does not appear to be a formal collaborative relationship between the various initiatives in OTD and the Center for Entrepreneurial studies.

Even so, a central challenge for UNC Chapel Hill would be how to better leverage its geographic and human capital endowments. The region's Research Triangle Park (RTP) offers robust high-tech research and development centers that serve as incubators for new ideas, as well as opportunities for entrepreneurial faculty and students to gain invaluable practical experience. UNC Chapel Hill should also continue to better cultivate and leverage the financial and professional support of successful alumni, entrepreneurs, and investors to provide a sustainable source of funding for innovative commercialization and entrepreneurship programs, as well as guidance to help it reach the market place.

Lastly, Ms. Judith Cone's comments will be instructive in better understanding UNC Chapel Hill's various innovative entrepreneurship, research, and technology transfer programs. As well as the impact of the NACIE commitment letter in framing UNC, Chapel Hill's strategic plans and institutional culture.

The Office of Innovation and Entrepreneurship thanks UNC, Chapel Hill's assistance with this case study, and looks forward to a continued close and collaborative relationship in building America's innovation infrastructure.

Entrepreneurship, Innovation, & Commercialization of Research at the Prairie View A&M University

Overview – Developing the Culture[28]

Prairie View A&M University (PVAMU) is a historically black university located in Prairie View, Texas, and is a member of the Texas A&M University System. PVAMU enrolls about 6,324 undergraduate students and 1,758 graduate students who come from all 50 U.S. states and several countries throughout the world. About 56% of the students are female, and 44% are male.

Dr. George C. Wright is the seventh President of Prairie View A&M University, the second oldest public institution of higher education in Texas. Under Dr. Wright's leadership, PVAMU continues to fulfill its land-grant mission of achieving excellence in teaching, research and service.

In 2011 PVAMU began a 3 to 5-year drive to improve innovation and research outputs in the university. There is now also an increasing recognition throughout the university community that the five buckets contained in the NACIE sponsored university commitment letter provides a blueprint to building successful entrepreneurship, innovation, and commercializing programs and culture.

An innate entrepreneurial culture among PVAMU students has also been a major catalyst for innovation programs. The university's strong engineering, science, technology, and nursing school have also been helpful.

Even so, PVAMU believes that an injection of "seed funding" access to U.S. government grants will encourage faculty to their research rate, and commercialization effort.

---

[28] Comments by: Dr. Rick Baldwin, Advisor, SIEF Program.

Below is an enumeration of Prairie View A&M University programs and initiatives that support the five buckets in the NACIE sponsored university commitment letter.

Student Entrepreneurship

Student In Free Enterprise - SIFE[lxxii]*: the Free Enterprise Institute* in Washington, D.C. has partnered with PVAMU students, since 1976, in several activities that promote free enterprise. The SIFE Team's programs inform and educate on the importance and benefits of the free enterprise system. These programs include the P-4 Investment Club, and sponsorships include the Personal Finance and Fiscal Fitness, Business Ethics, Student Entrepreneur and Business Expo, Entertainment Business Career Fair, Music Business Seminars, and the Changing the World Talent Showcase.

Framework for Opportunity Convergence and the Utilization of Sustainable Solutions (FOCUSS) Idea Competition[lxxiii] provides students a unique opportunity to share and cultivate creative solutions for sponsoring corporations. All current Prairie View A&M students are eligible to participate. Johnson Controls is a major corporate sponsor of the competition.

Faculty Entrepreneurship

There does not yet appear to be a formal arrangement to engage PVAMU faculty in entrepreneurship or commercialization of research initiatives. However, a number of PVAMU engagements appear to suggest an effort to engage both faculty and students in research and commercialization initiatives. These include:

The Center for Radiation Engineering and Science for Space Exploration (CRESSE)[lxxiv], a *NASA University Research Center* (URC) at PVAMU, uses its core intellectual, academic and physical infrastructure to thoroughly investigate the scientific and engineering challenges of space radiation. A better understanding and mitigation of radiation will help realize America's goal to someday safely return scientists, engineers and explorers to space destinations including Near Earth Asteroids (NEAs), Mars, and beyond.

- The prime objective of CRESSE is to merge new materials and technology into innovative radiation shielding systems.
- These shielding systems will keep critical electronic and scientific instruments and astronauts safe from harmful radiation, during future robotic and human missions into deep space.

Research Focus: Through September 2013, CRESSE research will focus on reliability issues during future NASA lunar and Martian missions. Specific areas of focus will include the dependability of space flight instrumentation and the health and safety of astronauts.

The 2010 RAMP Conference[lxv]—Research Association of Minority Professors— hosted by PVAMU sought to identify the University's role in enhancing faculty research in education, engineering, health and technology. The conference suggested several incentives to improve faculty research. These include:

- Granting faculty additional release time from teaching
    - Typical faculty teaching load is 12 semester;
    - Grant may provide 25% released time; and
    - University will grant a limited number of faculty an additional 25% release time for one semester or $3,000 to $6,000 to support faculty development.

University Technology Transfer Functions

PVAMU technology transfer functions are handled through its parent institution: *the Texas A&M University System Office of Technology Commercialization* (OTC)[lxxvi]. In fiscal year 2010 OTC achieved the following milestones:

- Licensing revenue generated by the Office of Technology Commercialization exceeded $8.5 million;
- The A&M System filed 65 new U.S. and foreign patent applications;
- 30 U.S. patents were issued based on A&M System technologies;
- A&M System entered into 46 new license agreements for the development of technologies; and
- On average, OTC staff processed 4 new disclosures per week

University-Industry Collaboration

Since 2004, the *Prairie View A&M University Small Business Development Center*[lxxvii] (PVAMU SBDC) has provided free consulting and assistance to businesses in Waller and Grimes counties. Services are extended to both start-ups and businesses seeking to scale-up. PVAMU SBDC professional consultants have extensive experience working with businesses in a wide variety of industries and bring practical knowledge and business expertise, from marketing to financial strategy.

Regional and Local Economic Development

Communi-Versity Economic Development Initiative[lxxviii] is a first-of-its kind economic development strategy for the City of Prairie View, which is home to Prairie View A&M University. Communi-Versity Advisory Council is comprised of leaders from the Prairie View community, PVAMU, and the private sector.

The Advisory Council works collaboratively with local city officials and economic development professionals to create jobs and attract additional business and investments that benefit both the university and the local community.

Deep-Dive Questions

- Is innovation an integral part of PVAMU's institutional culture?
- Why is it important? And how does it influence entrepreneurship and tech transfer?
- How do you envision your program in the future?
- What is your vision for each of the case study's bucket?
- How does your institution leverage (or intend to leverage) geographic endowment?
- Are your innovation, entrepreneurship, and tech transfer programs integrated? – Why, or why not?
- Are there any unique successes (and or challenges) you may wish to highlight?

Conclusion

The Center for Radiation Engineering and Science for Space Exploration (CRESSE) at the Prairie View A&M University is an example of the promise that the University's engineering pedigree holds in its quest to enhance student and faculty innovation and entrepreneurship. PVAMU's affiliation with the Texas A&M University System should also provide resources as well as give credibility to innovation and entrepreneurship initiatives.

Comments by Dr. Rick Baldwin have been instructive in better understanding Prairie View A&M University's quest for expanded innovative entrepreneurship, research, and technology transfer programs. It has framed the impact of the NACIE commitment letter by way of PVAMU's strategic plans and institutional culture.

The Office of Innovation and Entrepreneurship thanks Prairie View A&M University's assistance with this case study, and looks forward to a continued close and collaborative relationship in building America's innovation infrastructure.

Entrepreneurship, Innovation, & Commercialization of Research at the William Marsh Rice University (Rice), Houston, Texas

Overview—Commercializing Innovative Business Plans[29]

William Marsh Rice University - commonly referred to as Rice University or just Rice - is a private research university located in Houston, Texas. Since its establishment in 1912, Rice has grown into a highly regarded research university with an expanding entrepreneurship program.

Rice is noted for applied science programs in the fields of artificial heart research, structural chemical analysis, signal processing, space science, and nanotechnology. It was ranked first in the world in materials science research by the Times Higher Education (THE) in 2010[lxix]. Under the leadership of President David W. Leebron, Rice has maintained a very high level of research activity for its size, with $115.3 million[lxxx] in sponsored research funding in 2011.

Activities that support commercialization of research have also become a hallmark of Rice University. By the late 1990s, it became clear to a Rice University business professor that entrepreneurship and research programs at Stanford University and MIT were economic development catalysts in the Silicon Valley and greater Boston regions, respectively. Consequently, Rice decided that it had a duty and academic pedigree to replicate the human capital and economic development successes in the Houston, Texas region. With seed funding by former Rice president, Dr. S. Malcolm Gillis, their entrepreneurship program, known as the Rice Alliance for Technology and Entrepreneurship that brings together the George R. Brown School of Engineering, the Wiess School of natural sciences and the Jesse H. Jones Graduate School of Business in a strategic collaboration, opened in 2000.

Rice University maintains a "*distributive*" culture, which reflects the need to work across different arenas of campus, while consciously avoiding duplication. It also encourages bottom-up thinking and strategies. However, most innovation, entrepreneurship, and commercialization of research results,

[29] Comments by Brad Burke, Managing Director, Rice Alliance for Technology and Entrepreneurship.

transition through the Rice Alliance. This includes the just concluded 2012 *Rice Business Plan Competition.* The competition attracted 131 sponsors, 207 judges, and 42 graduate student teams who competed for $1.5million in prize money. The U.S. Department of Energy's Clean Energy Prize was one of the sponsors. 11 different schools have won the competition's grand prize in the last 12 years. In this way, the NACIE commitment letter is consistent with Rice University's culture of innovative approach to entrepreneurship and commercialization of research.

Brad Burke is the Executive Director of the Rice Alliance, and he reports to four different people—the heads of engineering, bio sciences, business school, and the vice president for research. The culture at Rice Alliance is favorably biased towards business plan competitions, rather than innovation competitions. Unlike business plan competitions, innovation competitions tend to promote innovation as an end, rather than a means. At Rice, the primary motivation for business plan competitions is to bring ideas to market; innovation at Rice University is a means to commercialization ends.

The number and acquisition value for some Rice Alliance business plan competitors have been impressive. 128 competitors have successfully launched companies, and 7 have exited through acquisitions. The 2005 Rice Business Plan Competition winner, *Auditude*, was acquired by Adobe for a reported $120 Million. Auditude also spun out another company, *IntoNow*, which was acquired in April 2011, by Yahoo, for a reported total value of $20 to $30 million.

Rice University adopts several eligibility standards that serve as the rule of thumb for business plan competitions applicants. Winners of the competition, which now serve as both catalyst and support structure, receive about $100,000 in seed funding. Participants are early stage companies, who may not have received over $500,000 in venture funding, and are seeking funding to develop commercial prototype. However, most teams have received some level of federal funding.

Rice considers itself one of the first universities to institute a university-wide entrepreneurship center. And the Rice Business Plan Competition provides students excellent experiential education. But there have been some drawbacks and challenges. The competition is on some level a victim of its success. The size and scope of the competition now requires increasingly more resources. Even so, Rice continues to seek innovative ways to ensure that every engineering student has some awareness of commercialization and entrepreneurship.

Other challenges abound. While many faculty members at Rice have a strong culture of entrepreneurship, overall, faculty feel they can improve on the 3 or 4 companies they commercialize annually. Faculty can also more effectively draw connections between their research and the creation of societal impact. There is a widespread concern that America is losing its global leadership position in research and commercialization. Government for its part should continue to improve policy and programs that promote innovation, entrepreneurship, and commercialization of technology. The Office of Innovation & Entrepreneurship's university case studies are a good start. Even so, especially because of its strong focus on research and commercialization, these remain the types of drawbacks and challenges the Rice Alliance is happy to engage. Houston's regional and local economy, for instance, derives invaluable benefits when Rice University convenes next generation companies.

In 2012 Rice Alliance will, in addition to the just completed Business Plan Competition, host the *2012 Energy & Clean Technology Venture Forum, and the 2012 IT and Web 2.0 Venture Forum*, among several other events. Rice University has also been severally recognized for its commitment to innovation and commercialization. These include the 2011 & 2012: #14 Best U.S. Entrepreneurship Program – US News & World Report; and the 2011 NASDAQ OMX Center of Entrepreneurial Excellence Award, among others. Below is an enumeration of Rice University programs that support the five focus areas outlined in the NACIE sponsored university commitment letter.

Student Entrepreneurship

Rice University Technology Venture Challenge[lxxxi] is a business plan competition where undergraduate students submit business plans for new technology ventures. Ventures have ranged from a solar-powered electric vehicle, improved tools for liposuction, low-cost vision testing device for individuals from developing countries, improved dry-eye diagnostic tool, improved defibrillator to ensure proper placement, among others.

CoRE—Community of Rice Entrepreneurs is a Rice undergraduate student entrepreneurship club that founded the business competition which is open to all Rice undergraduate students. The competition is supported by the Rice Alliance for Technology and Entrepreneurship, the *Rice Center for Engineering Leadership* (RCEL), and *Finger Interests*, a local investment firm headed by Jerry Finger, who is also an Adjunct Professor in Management at the Jones Graduate School of Business.

- Teams compete for three cash prizes totaling $8,750; and
- The grand prize is $5,000 in cash. More than 25 judges from the Houston business and investment community evaluate the business plan presentations.

In 2011 *the Rice Alliance*[lxxxiv] awarded prizes to all eight engineering and science graduate students and post-doctoral fellows who presented a four-minute pitch on their research findings and commercial applications for promising nanotechnology research at Rice University.

The Rice University Business Plan Competition (RBPC) is the world's richest and largest (according to Rice), awarding more than $1.3 million in prizes; Over 133 past competitors are in business today having raised in excess of $394 million.

Since 2001, 133 RBPC teams have launched their companies and are still in business today, raising a total of nearly $400 million in funding[lxxxiii].

In April 2012, 42 teams from around the world competed in front of 250 judges for an expected $1.3 million in prizes.

There are also additional prizes for the *Elevator Pitch Video* competition.

The RBPC expects to award 9 Major Investment Prizes including:

- $150,000 Grand Prize Investment from The GOOSE Society of Texas;
- $100,000 from Kleiner Perkins Caufield & Byers Prize for Clean Tech Innovation;
- $100,000 from Greater Houston Partnership/Opportunity Houston Investment Prize - Life Science;
- $100,000 from Greater Houston Partnership/Opportunity Houston Investment Prize - Energy/IT/Nano Aerospace;
- $100,000 from DFJ Mercury Tech Transfer Investment Prize;
- $100,000 from Waste Management "Think Green" Investment Prize;
- $100,000 from OWL Judges Investment Prize;
- $100,000 from Department of Energy Clean Energy Prize; and
- $20,000 from Courageous Women Entrepreneurs Prize.

3 Day Startup is an entrepreneurship education program designed for university students with an emphasis on learning by doing.

- The idea is simple: start tech companies
- ver the course of three days

Faculty Entrepreneurship

Faculty Advisory Committee is one of the internal advisory bodies of the Rice Alliance for Technology and Entrepreneurship (Rice Alliance), a nationally-recognized initiative devoted to the support of technology commercialization, entrepreneurship education, and the launch of technology companies.

Faculty members also work closely with the Office of Technology Transfer to protect intellectual property developed by them during their pursuit of the university's mission of providing an unsurpassed educational experience to its students and serving the educational needs of the larger community.

Rice Innovation Management System (RIMS)[lxxxiv] is an on-line system by the Office of Technology Transfer that allows researchers, especially faculty, at Rice to disclose their research innovations electronically. This new technology is the first step that professors take to turning their inventions into a product or service. By using the new system, faculty members will be able to reap some of the financial benefits of their inventions, create opportunities to receive additional funding for research and also helps them coordinate with other researchers if there is more than one group working on an invention.

University Technology Transfer Functions

The Rice Office of Technology Transfer (OTT)[lxxxv] is a component of the University's outreach efforts to make the benefits of new discoveries available to the public. OTT provides a service to Rice faculty members, students and staff researchers by protecting intellectual property developed by them.

- The OTT facilitates the interaction between academia and industry, so that science may be transformed into technology.

The Rice Alliance for Technology and Entrepreneurship (Rice Alliance)[lxxxvi] is Rice University's nationally-recognized initiative devoted to the support of technology commercialization, entrepreneurship education, and the launch of technology companies. It was formed as a strategic alliance of three schools: the George R. Brown School of Engineering, the Wiess School of Natural Sciences and the Jesse H. Jones Graduate School of Business in collaboration with the Vice Provost and the Office of Research.

- Since its inception in 2000, the Rice Alliance has assisted in the launch of more than 250 start-ups which have raised more than half a billion dollars in early-stage capital;

- More than 1000 companies have presented at the 125+ programs hosted by the Rice Alliance; and
- More than 26,000 individuals have attended Rice Alliance events in the past nine years and over 24,000 individuals subscribe to the Rice Alliance Digest newsletter.

University-Industry Collaboration

Rice University has initiatives that form part of its industry collaboration. These include: *The Virginia and L.E. Simmons Family Foundation Collaborative Research Fund*[lxxxvii]. The foundation generously provided $3 million over five years for collaborative research among investigators at Rice University, Texas Children's Hospital, and The Methodist Hospital Research Institute.

- The program is designed to promote truly excellent, collaborative, and interdisciplinary research among investigators at the three institutions; and
- The program focuses on junior investigators who have not yet established funding as well as experienced investigators who are new to collaboration among the three institutions

Rice's *Richard E. Smalley Institute for Nanoscale Science and Technology*[lxxxviii] has on-going research collaboration with nanoAlberta, part of Alberta Advanced Education and Technology in Canada, to address issues surrounding the production of petrochemicals from Alberta's oil sands, one of the world's largest reserves of recoverable oil.

Rice University is also one of *Texas Instrument's*[lxxxix] primary academic partners for research in embedded processing. Rice's digital signal processing (DSP) researchers recently won a new, three-year $1 million grant under the program.

Regional and Local Economic Development

Rice 360[oxc] draws on the diverse experience of faculty from the Jones School of Management, the Baker Institute of Public Policy, and the Schools of Social Sciences, Humanities, Natural Sciences, and Engineering to determine how to make technologies available, meaningful, and useful to people around the world. These technologies include a *low-cost incubator* designed Rice students that is with phototherapy lights based on the Blantyre

Hot Cot, which has been used in a Malawi hospital now for four years to treat babies with neonatal jaundice.

Deep - Dive Questions

- Is innovation an integral part of Rice's institutional culture?
- Why is it important? And how does it influence entrepreneurship and tech transfer?
- How do you envision your program in the future?
- What is your vision for each of the case study's bucket?
- How does your institution leverage (or intend to leverage) geographic endowment?
- Are your innovation, entrepreneurship, and tech transfer programs integrated?
  – Why, or why not?
- Are there any unique successes (and or challenges) you may wish to highlight?

Conclusion

Rice University is a leading private research University and an Association of American Universities (AAU) member school. Mr. Brad Burke's comments have been instructive in better understanding Rice's various innovative entrepreneurship, research, and technology transfer programs. It also frames the NACIE commitment letter by way of Rice University's strategic plans and institutional culture.

The Office of Innovation and Entrepreneurship thanks Rice's assistance with this case study, and looks forward to a continued close and collaborative relationship in building America's innovation infrastructure.

Entrepreneurship, Innovation, & Commercialization of Research at University of Southern California (USC)

Overview – Building an Innovation Community[30]

The University of Southern California (USC) is a private, not-for-profit, nonsectarian, research university located in Los Angeles, California. USC was founded in 1880, making it California's oldest private research university. The

[30] Comments by Krisztina "Z" Holly, former Vice Provost for Innovation, USC, & Executive Director, the USC Stevens Institute for Innovation.

university has a "very high" level of research activity, receiving $463.7 million in sponsored research between 2008 and 2009.

Dr. C. L. Max Nikias became the University of Southern California's eleventh president in August 2010. Dr. Nikias is the holder of the Robert C. Packard President's Chair and the Malcolm R. Currie Chair in Technology and the Humanities, and also chairs the USC Hospital's Governing Board. He holds faculty appointments in both electrical engineering and the classics[xci].

Not surprisingly, culture and community are important drivers of innovation at USC. Since innovation and entrepreneurship is ultimately about cultural change, university leadership works hard to drive community awareness of USC as an innovation "magnet." At USC, innovation is not an exclusive preserve of any school or center; a culture of innovation and entrepreneurship is promoted and celebrated campus wide without bias. Centers and institutes are not innovation silos but instead function as parts of a cohesive university community.

Ms. Krisztina "Z" Holly was vice provost for innovation at USC, and executive director of the USC Stevens Institute for Innovation, where she worked with academic units across USC to identify promising innovations and innovators, helping faculty and students make societal impact with their ideas. Z, a member of the National Advisory Council on Innovation and Entrepreneurship (NACIE), oversaw a diverse staff with expertise spanning business, marketing, financial and intellectual property management, technology licensing, and new venture creation[xcii].

In addition to being dispersed campus wide, innovation at USC is top-down/bottom-up agnostic. Innovative "garage" and "scalable" businesses alike are encouraged, especially among the student community. Consistent with USC's bottom-up approach, two USC seniors (Nathan Doctor and Reuben Fine) are helping entrepreneurially minded students connect with innovative companies who are seeking "out-of-the-box" thinkers. With support from entrepreneurial and engineering campus organizations, the seniors hosted a special event called the Entrepreneur Recruit at USC in April 2012. Another student driven innovation event is the recently concluded the USC Gamers Network presents: GAME ON 3, a semi-annual video game tournament.

Other competitions and events with industry partners abound. With assistance from innovation partner, PricewaterhouseCoopers (PwC), TEDxUSC 2012 will deliver an intellectual journey filled with brilliant speakers, captivating performances, amazing new technology, and thought-provoking short films. The theme for this year's event is "A Journey Through Spheres of Influence." Another industry sponsored event, Red Bull North

America's Game & Demo Lounge, will feature interactive tech demos, next generation video games, and a digital media art gallery.

TEDx, launched by USC in 2009, has become a global phenomenon. It has resulted in over 3,200 TEDx events in more than 90 countries and 40 different languages. TEDxUSC is produced and managed by the USC Stevens Institute for Innovation. These and several other USC innovation and entrepreneurship events have been invaluable in securing external stakeholder buy-in, as well as in enhancing USC's reputation as an innovation community.

Institutional agnosticism or at least recognition/accommodation of the tradeoffs, between top or bottom-driven innovation, and "garage" or "scalable" entrepreneurship have all been helpful in building USC's vibrant innovation culture. But ultimately, USC's success is attributable to university leadership's commitment to promoting an innovation culture within the university, while also establishing a reputation for the university as a "magnet" for innovation and entrepreneurship with the "right people" in the community. Otherwise innovation may just become brute force.

Below is an enumeration of USC's programs and initiatives that support the five buckets in the NACIE sponsored university commitment letter.

Student Entrepreneurship

The Center for Technology Commercialization (CTC)[xciii] at USC Marshall School of Business has several innovation and entrepreneurship programs for students.

- **MBA Commercialization Teams**: Through the *Technology Feasibility Course, the Ideas Empowered Program*, and by special request from researchers, CTC recruits MBA students to join researchers to conduct technology/market roadmaps, feasibility studies, and business design.
- **Internships**: Graduate and undergraduate students can apply for internships in startups through CTC's partnership with the *Business Technology Center* of the County of Los Angeles, and with USC alumni.
- CTC's academic component includes courses at the graduate level that prepare students to create new technology ventures.
- In conjunction with the *Lloyd Greif Center for Entrepreneurial Studies*, CTC offers a *Certificate in Technology Commercialization*; a four-course program open to matriculated and non-matriculated individuals in a graduate program or holding a graduate degree. This

university certificate is designed to give applicants a specialty in technology commercialization.

In addition to the certificate program in technology commercialization, USC Marshall School of Business also offers concentration in entrepreneurship and technology commercialization.

The *Entrepreneurship and Venture Management*[xciv] concentration at USC Marshall School of Business provides students with a thorough grounding in the business skills needed to start or manage a rapidly growing business. The courses offered not only give students the skills to excel in established industry roles; they also give the students the ability to spot and take full advantage of opportunities in small firms.

The *Technology Commercialization* concentration at USC Marshall School of Business prepares students to work in a variety of careers associated with technology commercialization. These include managing technology development projects; intellectual property or project portfolio; consulting to companies seeking to derive new revenue streams off archived IT; consulting to companies in the areas of technology and market feasibility; and managing commercialization effort. In addition, the concentration prepares the entrepreneur to take a technology from idea to market with in-depth and real-world knowledge of the technology commercialization process.

The *USC Entrepreneurship Club* (eClub)[xcv] helps students learn about entrepreneurship and launch their companies or ideas outside of the classroom, regardless of their major. For over a decade, the organization has served as an entrepreneurship hub for students and alumni. The eClub is also committed to organizing highly valuable and innovative events, while creating a support structure of resources, networks, and opportunities for startup and existing businesses.

The *USC Student Innovator Showcase and Competition*[xcvi] presented by the USC Stevens Institute for Innovation, is a university-wide innovator showcase which gives parents and students a highly interactive glimpse into the imaginations of USC student innovators, and a sneak peek at tomorrow's world. The showcase is hosted each year during the opening day of Trojan Family weekend and is followed by an awards reception (which includes cash prizes).

Faculty Entrepreneurship

The *Lloyd Greif Center for Entrepreneurial Studies*[xcvii] develops, supports, and disseminates leading-edge interdisciplinary scholarship on entrepreneurship. Among other programs and services, the Center provides research support to faculty members for entrepreneurship-related projects through its annual *Faculty Research Awards*. In 2011, the Greif Center awarded three faculty research grants totaling $11,000. Other programs include:

- *The Greif Seminar Series* brings leading entrepreneurship researchers to the Marshall School to present their recent work;
- *Greif-sponsored Conferences* bring together academics from around the world to present and discuss recent research; and
- *The Greif Research Impact Award* is a $5,000 annual award given to the researcher(s) who publishes the most impactful entrepreneurship article in top management and entrepreneurship journals.

The James H. Zumberge Research and Innovation Fund[xcviii] is USC's university-wide faculty research grant support mechanism. It awards several hundred thousand dollars each year through its annual James H. Zumberge Awards competition. The Zumberge Fund promotes the initiation of research at USC through two types of awards: Individual Awards and Interdisciplinary Awards. Recipients of Zumberge Interdisciplinary grants also derive these added benefits:

- Individual Awards help newer faculty launch their research careers, and support research in areas with limited external funding opportunities through grants of up to $25,000;
- Interdisciplinary Awards of up to $50,000 foster collaborative efforts among faculty from different schools and disciplines that lead to sustained interdisciplinary research programs and projects;
- $5 million per year in support from the *National Science Foundation's Science and Technology Center* program, to establish the *Center on Dark Energy Biosphere Investigations* at USC; and
- More than $4 million per year from the National Institutes of Health to bring the Bioinformatics Research Network (BIRN) to USC.

University Technology Transfer Functions

The USC Stevens Institute for Innovation is a university-wide resource in the Office of the Provost designed to harness and advance creative thinking and breakthrough research at USC for societal impact. The Stevens Institute nurtures, protects, and transfers the most exciting new innovations from USC to the market and thus provides a central connection for industry seeking cutting-edge innovations in which to invest.

The Stevens Institute develops the innovator as well as innovations, through educational programs, community-building events, and showcase opportunities. From the biosciences and technology, to music and cinematic arts, USC Stevens connects faculty, students, and the business community to create an environment for stimulating and inspiring innovation across all disciplines.

The *Alfred E. Mann Institute for Biomedical Engineering* (AMI)[xcix] at USC facilitates a faculty-welcoming process to help inventors mature their creations so that they can be transformed into commercially-viable medical products that help people and generate successes for inventors.

Beginning with a free consultation, AMI USC professionals provide a range of services for investors and companies including:

- Information on how to start a new own company;
- Detailed education on the commercialization process;
- Intellectual Property (IP) evaluation and market analysis; and
- Comprehensive assistance to inventors with the entire process of maturing their inventions for commercialization.

The Center for Technology Commercialization (CTC)[c] at the USC Marshall School of Business mission is to identify, encourage, and support technology entrepreneurship activities among faculty, students, and staff. CTC assists in the areas of IP issues, business feasibility analysis, business design, start-up financing, management team acquisition, preparation for funding, and related issues.

University-Industry Collaboration

USC welcomes industry collaboration to commercialize research, nurture startups, attract and motivate commercialization talent, and educate and train a world-class workforce.

The *Ideas Empowered Program*[ci] completed its pilot year in 2010. The program provides rigorous mentoring, programmatic support, and more than $450,000 in proof of concept funding to seven breakthrough ideas that have the potential to spinout of USC within two years. One of these projects, Cred.FM - led by USC School of Cinematic Arts professor and Co-founder of the EA Game Innovation Lab at USC, Chris Swain, has already completed their proof of concept within a year of participation in the program and will soon launch a beta of their social networking music sharing game.

The USC Viterbi School of Engineering, Keck School of Medicine of USC, the USC Stevens Institute for Innovation, and the Los Angeles Basin Clinical Translational Science Institute (CTSI) have been selected to participate in the exclusive Coulter Translational Research Partnership Program. Announced in April 2011, the prestigious program awards pioneering institutions that are fostering tomorrow's translational technologies and innovations in biomedical health care. The ultimate goal of this partnership is to focus on outcomes that will save, extend, and improve patient lives.

Johnson & Johnson and the USC Stevens Institute for Innovation, joined forces to form the USC – JNJ Translational Innovation Partnership Program[cii], designed to more rapidly develop early stage health science and medical technologies. Johnson & Johnson's Corporate Office of Science and Technology (COSAT) will provide $250,000 over two years. The USC Stevens Institute will lead a joint USC / JNJ COSAT review committee to identify groundbreaking ideas developed by USC's faculty for funding through this program. The program is structured to create a collaborative environment between academic and industry peers.

TEDxUSC has become a global phenomenon. TEDxUSC has been one of the most sought after, inspiring, jaw dropping, and entertaining conferences hosted by the University of Southern California. The presenter line-ups fascinate and delight guests, with mind-blowing technology demos, captivating talks, and stirring musical performances. Since creating TEDxUSC in March of 2009 and distributing the best practices, more than 2000 TEDx events have taken place in more than 90 countries and 37 different languages. Corporate partners have included PricewaterhouseCoopers and Red Bull USA, among others.

The USC Stevens Institute will continue outreach to partner with stellar private companies to fund and develop technology translation.

Regional and Local Economic Development

The University of Southern California leverages its unique relationships with industry, government, and nonprofits to spur economic development and encourage innovation across campus and throughout the nation.

An independent economic study suggests that USC generates $4.9 billion annually in economic activity in the Los Angeles region and beyond[ciii]. By December, 2008, USC produced about $2.1 billion dollars in total direct spending: wage and payroll expenditures of $1 billion, capital projects spending of $130 million and various purchasing expenditures of $430 million. Students spent another $503 million for goods and services, while visitors to USC spent about $12 million in the region. For every dollar spent by USC in Los Angeles County, an additional 63 cents of output was created elsewhere in the regional economy.

Capital improvement projects at USC also provide economic benefits for the City of Los Angeles, Los Angeles County, and the immediate community. The new housing at the Village at USC will provide more options to host a greater number of USC students, faculty and staff within walking distance of campus. The university-owned area north of campus, including the new Village development, will provide housing for up to 5,200 students and 250 faculty/student family apartments in a variety of housing types including studios to four bedroom units.

- Crucially construction of the Village at USC is expected to provide economic gains:
- 12,000 new jobs (4,000 construction-related, 8,000 permanent) throughout the Specific Plan development area;
- $1.1 billion construction-related economic impact on the Los Angeles County economy;
- $2.8 million in one-time construction revenue for the City of Los Angeles;
- $1.7 million in annual revenue benefits for the City of Los Angeles from The Village of USC operations; and
- $3.8 million in tax increment to the Community Redevelopment Agency through the year 2030; this is the single largest addition of tax increment revenue in South Los Angeles.

These are just but some of the several ways activities at USC drives and benefits the regional economy.

Deep-Dive Questions

- Is innovation an integral part of USC's institutional culture?
- Why is it important? And how does it influence entrepreneurship and tech transfer?
- How do you envision your program in the future?
- What is your vision for each of the case study's bucket, especially regional and local economic impact?

- How does your institution leverage (or intend to leverage) geographic endowment?
- Are your innovation, entrepreneurship, and tech transfer programs integrated?
  – Why, or why not?
- How has USC's one university in many places (multiple campus & online) model hindered or helped faculty and student innovation?
- Are there any unique successes (and or challenges) you may wish to highlight?

Conclusion

The University of Southern California (USC) is a private, not-for-profit, research university and an Association of American Universities (AAU) member school. Ms. Krisztina "Z" Holly's comments have been instructive in better understanding USC's various innovative entrepreneurship, research, and technology transfer programs. As well as the impact of the NACIE commitment letter in framing USC's strategic plans and institutional culture.

The Office of Innovation and Entrepreneurship thanks USC's assistance with this case study, and looks forward to a continued close and collaborative relationship in building America's innovation infrastructure.

End Notes

i. http://sports.espn.go.com/espn/commentary/news/story?id=6492198
ii. http://arkansasbaptist.edu/?page_id=1330
iii. http://arkansasnews.com/tag/arkansas-baptist-college/
iv. http://www.arkindcolleges.org/member-news/arkansas-baptist-college/news-story-headline/
v. http://sports.espn.go.com/espn/commentary/news/story?id=6492198
vi. http://coba.alasu.edu/ce_intlbusiness.html
vii. http://www.cobanetwork.com/sbdc/
viii. http://www.alasu.edu/news/news-details/index.aspx?nid=736
ix. http://ui.asu.edu/whatisui/?ui=0
x. http://studentventures.asu.edu/about
xi. http://innovationchallenge.asu.edu/
xii. http://theatrefilm.asu.edu/initiatives/pave/
xiii. http://10000solutions.org/
xiv. http://www.asu.edu/vppa/statelocal/files/2012_legislative_briefing_.pdf
xv. http://entrepreneurship.asu.edu/find-funding/faculty-staff-grants
xvi. https://asunews.asu.edu/20080717_techtransfer
xvii. http://www.fiercebiomarkers.com/story/5m-collaboration-cv-biomarkers/2011-11-02
xviii. http://www.asu.edu/vppa/statelocal/files/2012_legislative_briefing_.pdf
xix. www.forbes.com/2010/04/16/technology-incubators-changing-the-world-entrepreneurs-technology-incubator_slide_9.html

xx. http://www.gatech.edu/vision
xxi. http://www.ece.gatech.edu/research/labs/GE_Smartgrid
xxii. http://www.gatech.edu/newsroom/release.html?nid=66014
xxiii. http://www.industry.gatech.edu/about/about-ical/
xxiv. http://www.usg.edu/news/release/economic_impact_of_university_system_reaches_13.2_billion
xxv. http://www.gatech.edu/budgetupdate/economics.html
xxvi. http://www.theeliinstitute.org/business-plan-a-case-competitions/business-plan-competition
xxvii. http://www.theeliinstitute.org/business-plan-a-case-competitions
xxviii. http://www.theeliinstitute.org/courses-in-entrepreneurship
xxix. http://www.keadworks.com/
xxx. http://www.kojami.com/
xxxi. http://www.theeliinstitute.org/research
xxxii. http://www.howard.edu/research/index.html
xxxiii. http://ip.howard.edu/
xxxiv. http://ip.howard.edu/current_inventions.html
xxxv. http://smartlighting.rpi.edu/resources/PDFs/SmartLightingERC_Brochure_Web.pdf
xxxvi. http://www.quateams.com/aboutUs_news05_25.html
xxxvii. http://www.howard.edu/calendar/main.php?calendarid=default&view=event&eventid=1196799067703&timebegin=2007-12- 06+00%3A00%3A00
xxxviii. http://www.georgetownhowardctsa.org/
xxxix. http://www.bschool.howard.edu/deansmessage.htm
xl. http://www.dcsbdc.org/DocumentMaster.aspx?doc=1001
xli. http://www.coas.howard.edu/hucup/commdevleadership.html
xlii. http://net.educause.edu/ir/library/pdf/ff0710s.pdf
xliii. http://cra.gmu.edu/pdfs/researach_reports/recent_reports/Economic_Impacts_of_Howard_University.pdf
xliv. http://www.lorainccc.edu/About+Us/
xlv. http://www.lorainccc.edu/Academic+Divisions/Engineering+Technologies/Fab+Lab/
xlvi. Ibid
xlvii. http://www.lorainccc.edu/Faculty+and+Staff/Entrepreneurship/Student+IF+Information.htm
xlviii. http://www.lorainccc.edu/Business+and+Industry/At+Work+for+Business/Manufacturing/Advanced+Manufacturing.htm
xlix. http://www.lorainccc.edu/Faculty+and+Staff/Entrepreneurship/if+faculty.htm
l. http://www.lorainccc.edu/About+Us/Press+Releases+2009/Skills-Certification.htm
li. http://www.lorainccc.edu/Business+and+Industry/At+Work+for+Business/Manufacturing/Advanced+Manufacturing.htm
lii. http://www.lcccproud.com/community/dr-roy-a-church-of-lorain-county-community-college-to-receive-h-peter-burg-regional-visionaward
liii. http://www.lorainccc.edu/About+Us/Press+Releases+2011/White+House+Endorses+Launch+of+Innovation+Fund+America.htm
liv. http://www.techtransfer.umich.edu/
lv. http://innovate.umich.edu/u-m_programs/u-ms-entrepreneurial-ecosystem/
lvi. http://bec.umich.edu/index/
lvii. http://innovate.umich.edu/u-m_programs/u-ms-entrepreneurial-ecosystem/
lviii. http://www.innovationandeducation.com/about-the-authors
lix. http://www.lib.unc.edu/ncc/ref/unc/cq/kuralt.html
lx. http://www.kenan-flagler.unc.edu/entrepreneurship.aspx
lxi. http://otd.unc.edu/
lxii. http://www.kenan-flagler.unc.edu/entrepreneurship/programs#launching

lxiii. http://www.kfpefund.com/images/uploads/UNC_Kenan-Flagler_B-School_Gets_100K_Grant_from_Z_Capital,_James_Zenni_|_|_ peHUBpeHUB.pdf
lxiv. http://www.kenan-flagler.unc.edu/programs/mba/concentrations/entrepreneurship.aspx
lxv. http://otd.unc.edu/starting_a_company.php
lxvi. http://otd.unc.edu/OTDInterns.php
lxvii. http://www.cednc.org/content/about+ced/10063
lxviii. http://www.ncbiotech.org/about-us
lxix. http://www.sbtdc.org/about-us/
lxx. http://www.ncidea.org/
lxxi. http://www.unc.edu/campus-updates/innovateCarolina
lxxii. http://www.pvamu.edu/pages/1865.asp
lxxiii. http://www.foc-uss.com/ideacompetition-prairieview-johnsoncontrols.html
lxxiv. http://www.nasa.gov/offices/education/programs/national/urc/group_IV/pvamu.html
lxxv. http://www.pvamu.edu/Include/research/Presentations/2010%20RAMP%20Conference.pdf
lxxvi. http://otc.tamu.edu/about/stats.jsp
lxxvii. http://www.pvamu.sbdcnetwork.net/prairieview/Who_we_are.asp
lxxviii. http://www.teex.com/teex.cfm?pageid=media&area=teex&templateid=23&storyid=1024
lxxix. http://www.timeshighereducation.co.uk/story.asp?sectioncode=26&storycode=410831
lxxx. http://www.professor.rice.edu/professor/Research_Revenues.asp
lxxxi. http://rbpc.rice.edu/RA2011_2Column.aspx?id=787
lxxxii. http://rbpc.rice.edu/RA2011_2Column.aspx?id=782
lxxxiii. http://alliance.rice.edu/rbpc.aspx
lxxxiv. http://ott.rice.edu/news/NewsDetail.cfm?NewsID=21
lxxxv. http://ott.rice.edu/news/NewsDetail.cfm?NewsID=13
lxxxvi. http://alliance.rice.edu/about/
lxxxvii. https://www.collaborativeresearchfund.org/
lxxxviii. http://www.azocleantech.com/news.aspx?newsID=6657
lxxxix. http://www.ti.com/corp/docs/webemail/2008/enewsltr/public-affairs/jul08/landing/education2.shtml
xc. http://www.rice360.rice.edu/content.aspx?id=40&linkidentifier=id&itemid=40
xci. http://www.president.usc.edu/short-bio/
xcii. http://www.provost.usc.edu/senior-administration/krisztina-z-holly/
xciii. http://www.marshall.usc.edu/faculty/centers/ctc/about
xciv. http://classic.marshall.usc.edu/ecg/concentrations/entrepreneurship-program.htm#Entrepreneurship_and_Venture_Management
xcv. http://www.eclubusc.com/?page_id=41
xcvi. http://stevens.usc.edu/studentinnovatorshowcase.php
xcvii. http://www.marshall.usc.edu/faculty/centers/greif/research
xcviii. http://research.usc.edu/for-investigators/funding/usc/zumberge/
xcix. http://ami.usc.edu/launchpad.php
c. http://www.marshall.usc.edu/faculty/centers/ctc/about
ci. http://stevens.usc.edu/ideasempowered.php
cii. http://stevens.usc.edu/JNJinnovationfund.php
ciii. http://news.usc.edu/#!/article/26426/USC-Has-Nearly-5-Billion-Economic-Impact

In: The Role of Higher Education in Innovation ISBN: 978-1-63321-176-6
Editor: Armando M. Clinton

Chapter 2

STATEMENT OF CHARLES O. HOLLIDAY, CHAIR, COMMITTEE ON RESEARCH UNIVERSITIES, THE NATIONAL RESEARCH COUNCIL. HEARING ON "THE ROLE OF RESEARCH UNIVERSITIES IN SECURING AMERICA'S FUTURE PROSPERITY: CHALLENGES AND EXPECTATIONS"*

INTRODUCTION

Good morning, Mr. Chairman and members of the Subcommittee on Research and Science Education. My name is Chad Holliday. I am the retired Chair and CEO of DuPont and currently serve as non-executive Chairman of the Board of Bank of America. I am testifying to you today in my capacity as Chair of the Committee on Research Universities of the National Research Council (NRC). The Research Council is the operating arm of the National Academy of Sciences, National Academy of Engineering, and the Institute of Medicine of the National Academies, chartered by Congress in 1863 to advise the government on matters of science and technology. The Council's Committee on Research Universities released its report, *Research Universities*

---

* This is an edited, reformatted and augmented version of a statement presented June 27, 2012 before the House Committee on Science, Space and Technology, Subcommittee on Research and Science Education.

and the Future of America: Ten Breakthrough Actions Vial to Our Nation's Prosperity and Security, on June 14, 2012, and you have asked me to appear before you today to provide you an overview of its findings and recommendations.

CONTEXT

Mr. Chairman, America in the 21st century is driven by innovation – that is, advances in ideas, products, and processes that create new industries and jobs, contribute to our nation's health and security, and allow us to achieve our national goals. Innovation in the United States, in turn, has been increasingly driven by educated people and the knowledge they produce. And our nation's primary source of both new knowledge and graduates with advanced skills is our nation's research universities. As such, this set of institutions represent a key asset—perhaps even our most potent national asset—for the 21st century.

Today, 35 to 40 of the top 50 research universities in the world are in the United States. And the strength of these institutions, public and private, is the direct result of forward-looking federal and state policies, largely enacted by Congress and often in periods of national crisis. Indeed, we can begin this story almost exactly 150 years ago during the Civil War with the enactment of the Morrill Land-Grant College Act of 1862 that established a partnership between the federal government and the states to build universities that would address the challenges of creating a modern agricultural and industrial economy. The story continues with the strengthening of this partnership during and following World War II: over the last 60 years, federal policies and programs have concentrated basic research in our universities and funded it through federal programs that have supported a unique and extremely productive combination of research and graduate education.

In 2009, Representatives Bart Gordon and Ralph Hall, then Chair and Ranking Member of the House Science Committee, and Senators Lamar Alexander and Barbara Mikulski requested that the National Academies prepare, as a follow-up to the landmark *Rising Above the Gathering Storm*, a report examining more deeply the health and competitiveness of the nation's research universities. In their letter of request, they noted that America's research universities "have been the critical assets that have laid the groundwork—through research and doctoral education—for the development of many of the competitive advantages that make possible the high American standard of living." But they were also alarmed that while our research universities consistently rank among the best in the world they are nevertheless "under stress, even as other countries are measurably improving the quality of their research institutions."

Indeed, our research universities today confront challenges and opportunities that require systematic response. Consequently, the Congressional request asked that the NRC assess the competitive position of our research universities and respond to the following question:

> What are the top ten actions that Congress, state governments, research universities, and others can take to maintain the excellence in research and doctoral education needed to help the United States compete, prosper, and achieve national goals for health, energy, the environment, and security in the global community of the 21st century?

In response, the NRC convened a committee of leaders in academia, industry, government, and national laboratories.1 That committee has now delivered its report, Research Universities and the Future of America: *Ten Breakthrough Actions Vital to Our Nation's Prosperity and Security.*

KEY FINDINGS

Research Universities and the Future of America argues that the nation must reaffirm and revitalize the unique partnership that has long existed among research universities, federal and state governments, and philanthropy, and strengthen its links with business. It is this partnership that is central to the global strength of our institutions and what makes them a potent asset for our nation. University research has addressed environmental concerns, such as damage to the earth's ozone shield; produced new drugs and technology that improve health, including synthetic insulin, blood thinners, and magnetic resonance imaging (MRI); led to innovations that make our nation safer, such as imaging technology that scans containers as they enter our ports; and contributed countless products that have revolutionized our way of life, including lasers, rocket fuel, computers, and key components of the World Wide Web. And talented graduates of these institutions have created and populated many new businesses that have employed millions of Americans.

Despite their success, our nation's research universities are now confronting challenges and opportunities that a reasoned set of policies must address in order to produce the greatest return to our society, our security, and our economy. Research Universities identified the following as especially important:

- Federal funding for university research has been unstable and, in real terms, declining at a time when other countries have increased funding for research and development (R&D). State funding for higher education, already eroding in real terms for more than two decades, has been cut further during the recent recession.
- Business and industry have largely dismantled the large corporate research laboratories that drove American industrial leadership in the 20th century (for example, Bell Labs), but have not yet fully partnered with research universities to fill the gap.
- Research universities must improve management, productivity, and cost efficiency in both administration and academics.
- Young faculty have insufficient opportunities to launch academic careers and research programs.
- There has been an underinvestment in campus infrastructure, particularly in cyberinfrastructure, that could lead to long-term increases in productivity, cost-effectiveness, and innovation in research, education, and administration.
- Research sponsors often do not pay the full cost of research they procure, which means that universities have to cross-subsidize sponsored research from other sources, such as tuition or clinical revenues.
- A burdensome accumulation of federal and state regulatory and reporting requirements increases costs and sometimes challenges academic freedom and integrity.
- Doctoral and postdoctoral preparation could be enhanced by shortening time-to-degree, raising completion rates, and enhancing programs' effectiveness in providing training for highly-productive careers.
- Demographic change in the U.S. population necessitates strategies for increasing the educational success of female and underrepresented minority students.

- Institutions abroad are increasingly competing for international students, researchers, and scholars, as other nations increase their investment in their own institutions.
- Research Universities argues that we must address these issues in order to assure that our institutions continue to contribute the new knowledge and talented people our society requires.

RECOMMENDATIONS

The report provides ten strategic recommendations requiring strong actions from the federal government, state governments, universities, and business that are designed to accomplish three broad goals: (i) strengthen the partnership among universities, federal and state governments, philanthropy, and business in order to revitalize university research and speed its translation into innovative products and services; (ii) improve the productivity of administrative operations, research, and education within universities; and (iii) ensure that America's pipeline of future talent in science, engineering, and other research areas remains creative and vital, leveraging the abilities of all of its citizens and attracting the best students and scholars from around the world.

The report provides actions to be taken by recommendation. Here I wish to review, instead, the actions to be taken by actor.

Universities

We call on universities in our report to play a strong role in shaping the future for themselves, for those they serve, and for the nation.

First and foremost, the nation's research universities should set and achieve bold goals in cost-containment, efficiency, and productivity in business operations and academic programs, striving to limit the cost escalation of all ongoing activities -- academic and auxiliary -- to the inflation rate or less. In addition to implementing efficient business practices, universities should (1) review existing academic programs from the perspectives of centrality, quality, and cost-effectiveness, (2) encourage greater collaboration among research investigators and among research institutions, particularly in acquiring and using expensive research equipment and facilities, (3) adopt modern instructional methods such as cyberlearning, and (4) improve management of intellectual property to improve technology transfer.

By increasing cost-effectiveness and productivity, institutions will realize significant cost-savings in operations that may be used to improve their performance, allowing them to shift resources strategically and/or reduce growth in their need for resources such as tuition. Many institutions have already demonstrated that significant cost efficiencies are attainable. University associations should develop and make available more powerful and strategic tools for financial management and cost accounting that enable universities to determine the most effective ways to contain costs and increase productivity and efficiency. As part of this effort, they should develop metrics that allow universities to communicate their level of cost-effectiveness to the general public.

In fulfilling their educational mission, research universities should engage in efforts to improve education for all students at all levels in the United States by reaching out to K-12 school districts and by taking steps to improve access and completion in their own institutions. Similarly, research universities should assist efforts to improve the education and preparation of those who teach STEM subjects in grades K-12. Universities should also strive to improve undergraduate education, including persistence and completion rates in STEM, and take urgent, sustained, and intensive action to increase the participation and success of women and underrepresented minorities. Research universities should also restructure doctoral education to enhance pathways for talented undergraduates, improve completion rates, shorten time-todegree, and strengthen the preparation of graduates for careers both in and beyond the academy.

State Governments

For states to compete for the prosperity and welfare of their citizens in a knowledge-driven global economy, the advanced education, research, and innovation programs provided by their research universities are absolutely essential. And the importance of these universities extends far beyond state borders; these institutions play a critical role in the prosperity, public health, and security of their regions and the entire nation. However, an alarming erosion in state support for higher education over the past decade has put the quality and capacity of public research universities at great risk. State cuts in appropriations to public research universities over the years 2002 to 2010 are estimated to average 25 percent -- and range as high as 50 percent for some universities -- resulting in the need for institutions to increase tuition or to reduce either activities or quality.

Going forward, state governments should move rapidly to provide their public research universities with sufficient autonomy and agility to navigate an extended period with limited state support. As budgets recover from the current recession, though, states should strive to restore and maintain per-student funding for higher education, including public research universities, to the mean level for the 15-year period 1987-2002, as adjusted for inflation. Federal programs designed to stimulate innovation and workforce development at the state level, including those recommended in this report, should be accompanied by strong incentives to stimulate and sustain state support for their public universities, which are both state and national assets.

Federal Action

The study committee was acutely aware of – and robustly discussed—the current federal fiscal environment and, consequently, recommends both actions with little or no cost that could be taken in the short term and increased investments that should be made over time as the economy improves.

Federal Policies on Costs and Regulation

There are important actions that could be taken – in fact should be taken – in a constrained budget environment. First, the federal government and other research sponsors should support the full cost, direct and indirect, of research and other activities they procure from universities so that it is no longer necessary to subsidize these sponsored grants by drawing on resources intended to support other important university missions, such as undergraduate education and clinical care. Both sponsored research policies and cost-recovery negotiations should be developed and applied in a consistent fashion across all federal agencies and academic institutions, public and private.

Second, federal policymakers and regulators (OMB, Congress, Agencies) and their state counterparts should review the costs and benefits of federal and state regulations, eliminating those that are redundant, ineffective, inappropriately applied to the higher education sector, or impose costs that outweigh the benefits to society. The federal government should also make regulations and reporting requirements more consistent across federal agencies so that universities can maintain one system for all federal requirements rather than several, thereby reducing costs. Reducing or eliminating regulations can reduce administrative costs, enhance productivity, and increase the agility of institutions. With greater resources and freedom, universities will be better positioned to respond to the needs of their constituents in an increasingly competitive environment.

Federal Investments

Over the next decade, as the economy improves, the federal government should invest in basic research, graduate education, infrastructure and technology transfer in order to produce the new knowledge and educated citizens the nation needs and to ensure that these are fully and productively deployed in our economy and society.

Congress and the administration should provide full funding of the amount authorized by the America COMPETES Act, doubling the level of basic research conducted by the National Science Foundation, National Institute of Standards and Technology, and the Department of Energy's Office of Science. By completing funding increases that Congress has already authorized, the nation would ensure robust support for critical basic research programs, achieving a balanced research portfolio capable of driving the innovation necessary for economic prosperity. Together with cost-efficient regulation, this stable funding will enable universities to make comparable investments in research facilities and graduate programs. And because research and education are intertwined in universities, this funding will also ensure that we continue to produce the scientists, engineers, and other knowledge professionals the nation needs.

The federal government should, within the context of also making the R&D tax credit permanent, implement new tax policies that incentivize business to develop partnerships with universities (and others as warranted) for research that results in new economic activities located in the United States.

The federal government should significantly increase its support for graduate education through balanced programs of fellowships, traineeships, and research assistantships provided by all science agencies that depend upon individuals with advanced training. This rebalancing of support is designed to facilitate better alignment of doctoral education with national needs and with the careers of graduates. Furthermore, all stakeholders – the federal government, states, local school districts, industry, philanthropy, and universities -- should take urgent, sustained, and intensive action to increase the participation and success of women and underrepresented minorities across all academic and professional disciplines, especially in science, mathematics, and engineering.

The federal government should create a new Strategic Investment Program to support two 10-year initiatives: (1) an endowed faculty chairs program to facilitate the careers of young investigators during a time of serious financial stress and limited faculty retirements, and (2) a research infrastructure program initially focused on rapidly evolving cyberinfrastructure that will increase productivity and collaboration in research and may also do so in administration and education. Federal investments in these initiatives would be intended for both public and private research universities, and they would require institutions to obtain matching funds from states, philanthropy, business, or other sources. Also of critical importance is the endowment of chairs, particularly for promising young faculty.

Federal agencies should ensure that visa processing for international students and scholars who wish to study or conduct research in the United States is as efficient and effective as possible consistent with homeland security considerations. In order to ensure that a high proportion of non-U.S. doctoral researchers remain in the country, the federal government should also streamline the processes for these researchers to obtain permanent residency or U.S. citizenship. The United States should consider taking the strong step of granting residency (a green card) to each non-U.S. citizen who earns a doctorate in an area of national need from an accredited research university.

Business Action

The role of business in the university-government-industry partnership is critically important and must be enhanced. As noted above, industry has largely dismantled the large corporate research laboratories that drove American industrial leadership in the 20th century (e.g., Bell Labs), but have not yet fully partnered with research universities to fill the gap. Nor have they adequately partnered with university programs to help produce the advanced graduates that industry needs.

Tax incentives and research support mechanisms can promote collaboration between business and universities that will lead to the creation and efficient use of knowledge to achieve national goals—particularly the development of new products and US-located economic activity and jobs. In order for this to be successful, the relationship between business and higher education should become more peer-to-peer in nature, stressing collaboration in areas of joint interest rather than remaining in a traditional customer-supplier relationship, in which business procures graduates and intellectual property from universities.

Businesses and universities should work closely together to develop new graduate degree programs that address strategic workforce gaps for science-based employers. Employers -- businesses, government agencies, and non-profits -- that hire master's and doctorate level graduates should more deeply engage programs in research universities by providing internships, student projects, advice on curriculum design, and real-time information on employment opportunities.

COMMITTEE PROCESS

The committee agreed to the above findings and recommendations following a rigorous process of information gathering and deliberation. As outlined in an appendix to the report, the committee solicited input for its study from a broad range of stakeholders during the course of several meetings. In parallel with our information gathering process, the committee deliberated its findings and conclusions by first considering the current strengths and weaknesses of our research universities and the opportunities and threats they face today and are likely to face over the next decade. This deliberation allowed the committee to brainstorm and discuss key issues over a period of time, including several committee meetings, and ultimately formulate the set of ten issues they agreed to address in the report.

The study committee reached consensus on the top ten report recommendations through thorough discussion that addressed strengths and opportunities, weaknesses and threats, but also difficult contextual issues that would affect actions and potential outcomes. These contextual issues included the current federal fiscal environment; pressures on state budgets over time; the intricacies of university finances, including cross-subsidies; increases in tuition, typically driven by pressures on other revenue streams; the kinds of productivity gains that universities can achieve, and under what scenarios; the appropriate roles of universities, government, and business in the development of technology and its transfer into the marketplace, and the importance of differences by industry; and the need for more effective communication of these complicated issues to the public. We were strongly motivated to present a mix of actions that were low-cost or no-cost as well as actions that required investments and we have done so. We believe we have presented a fair and balanced – as well as critically important – set of recommendations that require strong action from all key stakeholders in the university government-industry partnership.

Your written questions asked if there were issues that were particularly challenging for consensus building. There was a concern at the outset that one such issue might be differences between public and private research institutions over steps to be taken to develop a way forward from the current economic and fiscal climate. No such difference materialized and, indeed, I can report that the entire committee was strongly unanimous in their recommendations regarding the importance of ensuring the strength of our nation's public institutions that are critical not only to their states and regions, but also to the nation. Another, related issue that might have also raised differences of opinion was the rhetorical question about the "right number" of research universities in the United States. The committee did not believe any group of people could determine a priori what the "right number" of such institutions might be and that it would be damaging to try to do so. Instead, it is important to articulate a set of principles that would naturally lead to an appropriate, but fluid number: these include the importance of merit review, competition, and striving for excellence in faculty and students; they also include taking the opportunity to build capacity or incentivize regional partnerships when it makes sense for the benefit of the nation. The committee also believes that the ecosystem of research universities should be diverse. It will include large and comprehensive institutions that can aspire to excellence across the range of fields and others that, because of limited resources or a particular comparative advantage, should pick specific areas in which they should compete.

Lastly, I would like to note four additional items of national importance that came before us that we did not act on because other committees properly assembled for the task had been empanelled to do so. First, some members of the committee were interested in exploring the business model for research, particularly in the biomedical sciences. We did not take up this subject because the Advisory Committee to the Director of the National Institutes of Health had appointed a task force to examine the structure of the biomedical workforce and appeared to be ready to explore the issues raised before us.2 Second, a related issue focuses on the status, conditions, and future careers of the nation's postdoctoral trainees. We addressed this in an oblique way through our recommendations on reform of doctoral education and the creation of an endowed chairs program, but the postdoctoral experience requires more in-depth examination. During the course of our work, the National Academies appointed a study committee, under the aegis of the Committee on Science, Engineering, and Public Policy (COSEPUP) to undertake just that and we await their final report. Third, the Experimental Program to Stimulate Competitive Research (EPSCoR) and similar programs play a fundamental role in the research university landscape. We might have looked more in-depth at that program. However, during the course of our study Congress mandated that the Academies undertake an assessment of the EPSCoR program and the Academies have appointed a study committee to do that, also under the aegis of COSEPUP. Lastly, committee members were very concerned that the full range of fields in the research university—across the physical sciences, life sciences, engineering, social sciences, and humanities—be preserved as critical to the core mission of education and research. We were pleased to note in our report that, in response to a Congressional request similar to ours, that the American Academy of Arts and Sciences has appointed a blue-ribbon committee that will soon release a report on strengthening the humanities and social sciences in higher education and society. As you can imagine, the committee received in its meetings a large range of issues and recommendations from well-informed and engaged individuals, universities, and associations. While we could not include all of them, the committee's records in its Public Access File will preserve them for possible use by similar committees in the future.

CONCLUSION

Mr. Chairman, I would like to note again, in conclusion, that during past eras of challenge and change, our national leaders have acted decisively to create innovative partnerships to enable our universities to enhance American security and prosperity. Today our nation faces new challenges, a time of rapid economic, social, and political transformation driven by an exponential growth in knowledge and innovation. A decade into the 21st century, a resurgent America must stimulate its economy, address new threats, and position itself in a competitive world transformed by technology, global competitiveness, and geopolitical change. In this environment, educated people, the knowledge they produce, and the innovation and entrepreneurial skills they possess, particularly in the fields of science and engineering, are keys to our nation's future. So, it is essential that we reaffirm and revitalize the unique partnership that has long existed among the nation's research universities, federal government, states, philanthropy, and business. The actions recommended in our report will require significant policy changes, productivity enhancement, and investments on the part of each member of the research partnership. Yet they also comprise a fair and balanced program that will generate significant returns for a stronger America.

Mr. Chairman, thank you for this opportunity to address the Subcommittee on this set of issues so critical to our nation.

INDEX

C

D

E

F

G

H

I

J

K

L

M

R

S

T

U

V

W

Y